THE REACTIONARY MIND

The ReactiOnary Mind

WHY "CONSERVATIVE" ISN'T ENOUGH

Michael Warren Davis

REGNERY GATEWAY
Washington, D.C.

Regnery Gateway™ is a trademark of Salem Communications Holding Corporation
Regnery® is a registered trademark and its colophon is a trademark of Salem Communications Holding Corporation

Cataloging-in-Publication data on file with the Library of Congress

ISBN: 978-1-68451-132-7
eISBN: 978-1-68451-146-4
Library of Congress Control Number: 2021943478

Published in the United States by
Regnery Gateway, an Imprint of
Regnery Publishing
A Division of Salem Media Group
Washington, D.C.
www.Regnery.com

Manufactured in the United States of America

10 9 8 7 6 5 4 3 2 1

Books are available in quantity for promotional or premium use. For information on discounts and terms, please visit our website: www.Regnery.com.

For Helena

Well, if I have to choose one or the other
I choose to be a plain New Hampshire farmer.
—Robert Frost

Contents

The Happy Warrior

To be happy at home is the end of all human endeavor.
—Samuel Johnson

T his is a book about happiness.

Happiness is something we tend to take for granted. Which is odd, really. By every measurement, Americans are less happy than we've ever been in our country's history. More and more of us report feeling chronically lonely. We have fewer friends and less sex. Divorce rates are falling, but only because marriage rates are falling even faster. Meanwhile, deaths by despair are way up—so much so that the life expectancy for white males is declining for the first time in recorded history.

How can this be?

Here's my theory: for too long, we've confused happiness with comfort.

And we Americans are pretty damn comfortable. We have smart-phones and air conditioners. We have Tinder, Uber, and the drive-thru at McDonald's—all in one night, if you time it right. A friend of mine from Australia remembers his family getting dressed up every time they went to Sydney. "Even the beggars wore a coat and tie," he recalls. Today, we have athleisure.

We're comfortable, sure. But we're not happy.

As a matter of fact, I think some of us really chafe under all this comfort. That's the thesis of this book. It begins with the awesome, bracing revelation that grown-ups actually *like* doing things for themselves. We don't want to be constantly comforted and pampered. We don't want to be distracted by a constant stream of bright lights and inane noises. That's fine for babies, but not for men and women. It doesn't actually make us happy.

We want freedom. We want independence. And we know, if we're honest, that freedom and independence come only through struggle and strain.

But we haven't been honest; we've redefined freedom and independence. Freedom used to mean the ability to do what's right, free from unjust coercion. Today, it means doing whatever the hell you want. Justice Anthony Kennedy put it best in his majority decision for *Planned Parenthood v. Casey*: "At the heart of liberty is the right to define one's own concept of existence, of meaning, of the universe, and of the mystery of human life." And that's much easier, isn't it? For us, freedom is about making choices—the choice between Uber and Lyft, between McDonald's and Burger King. If you're really forward-thinking, it's the choice between Tinder and Grindr.

And independence? Well, that was all right in simpler times, but today life is complicated and best left to the professionals. An army of helpful bureaucrats stand ready to tell you what to eat, what to drink, and what books your children should read. There's an app to tell you whom to vote for, whom to marry, and (according to my uncle, a TikTok fiend) when to go to bed. A child born in the year 2021 could easily go his entire life without making a single consequential decision for himself.

Some might call that convenience. I call it slavery.

I'm not here to blame anyone. Not the Protestants or the Jacobins, the boomers or the millennials, not even the World Economic Forum. That's all way too simplistic. No, I blame me. And I blame you. Because the fact is that we *chose* slavery over freedom. For centuries now, we've been slowly trading away our independence and gladly selling off our happiness to Big Government, Big Business, and (lately) Big Tech—all in exchange for more creature comforts.

We renew that servitude about a hundred times every day. When we order T-shirts on Amazon instead of going to the store. When we grab a hot-and-ready pizza instead of cooking for ourselves. When we text our best friends instead of going down to the bar for a drink. When we flick through our phones on the bus instead of reading a book. When we stay up until midnight watching Steven Crowder absolutely *destroy* some dumb college freshman. When we cash our eighteenth COVID stimulus check, despite having been gainfully employed for ten years.

You know, there's a word for people who only talk to their friends over the phone, who have their clothes and their meals delivered right to their door, and who bill everything to the government. They're called prisoners. And that's what we've become. We're prisoners of our own convenience.

Think about it. When the coronavirus pandemic swept the United States, practically every governor in the country declared a state of "lockdown." Now, I don't know the first thing about health policy. What I do know is that the lockdown orders couldn't have happened twenty years ago; the very idea of putting virtually every American into solitary confinement would have been inconceivable. How could we all go into lockdown when everything happens *out there*? Except for new moms and small children, basically everyone was out of the house for most of the day. Folks couldn't imagine living any other way—until, of course, they could.

That was the real horror of the lockdown. It proved that a huge majority of Americans could get by in isolation. It's not that the government could tell us to stay home and we did. (That's another matter.) It's that it *worked*. There was no mass starvation. We ran low on beef and toilet paper, but the supply chain held up.

Apparently, Margaret Thatcher was right: there's no such thing as society. Not anymore. COVID checks, Amazon Prime, and Netflix made it redundant.

But is that how we want to live?

We thought that technology's making everyone more interconnected would bring human beings closer to one another. In fact, just the opposite has happened. All of our relationships have become shallower, more transactional. We use one another, but we don't really need one another. Once delivery drones and sex robots take off, we won't need other human beings for anything. Then we'll all be comfortable as hell.

But I ask you again: Is that what we really want? Will that make us happy?

It has taken the better part of seven hundred years for mankind to render itself redundant. This is a process we've (rather cruelly) dubbed "progress." The True, the Good, and the Beautiful came at too high a cost: our blood, sweat, and tears. We traded in beauty for the merely sensual. We gave up on goodness in favor of self-expression. Truth is out; ideology is in.

Part I of this book will consider the major catastrophes in Western history that brought about this false progress: the Renaissance, the Protestant Reformation, the Scientific Revolution, the Enlightenment, and the French Revolution.

We'll meet those heroic reactionaries who fought to stem the tide. These men stood for freedom and independence against servitude and decadence. They're partisans of truth, goodness, and beauty. These are men like Girolamo Savonarola, Thomas More, Robert Bellarmine, Joseph de Maistre, Ned Ludd, and G. K. Chesterton.

We'll also discuss how this idea of endless, unstoppable "progress" left us blind to the damage wrought over the last seven centuries and totally unable to imagine a better future for ourselves and our children.

Along the way, we'll see how "conservatives" have served as adagio progressives: accepting "progress," but slowly. The American journalist William F. Buckley Jr. famously declared that the conservative is one who "stands athwart history, yelling Stop." But that was more of an aspiration than a reality. In truth, conservatives always seem to wind up jogging alongside history, huffing, "Please, for the love of God, slow down." That's no coincidence. Nor is the fact that so many "conservatives" finally wear down and simply say, "Hurrah for progress! Hurrah for capitalism!" Not only is it easier to say that, but they lack the philosophical wherewithal to say anything else.

Part II is a handbook for would-be reactionaries. The reactionary lives in open revolt against the modern world. He believes in simplicity and piety, strength and sacrifice. He categorically rejects both politics and economics; he has no opinions, only principles. He minds his own business, though he strives to be useful to others.

The reactionary understands intuitively these lines from William Wordsworth:

> *The world is too much with us; late and soon,*
> *Getting and spending, we lay waste our powers;—*
> *Little we see in Nature that is ours;*
> *We have given our hearts away, a sordid boon!*

The reactionary's motto, if he has one, is simply this, from 1 Peter 2:17: "Honor all men. Love the brotherhood. Fear God. Honor the king."

Above all, perhaps, he's happy. He may be the last truly happy man on earth. He loves life because he surrounds himself with lovable things: family and friends, plants and animals, hearth and home. His work isn't a chore, and his leisure isn't mere distraction. He's constantly challenging himself—mind, body, and soul. He lives "loyally and joyfully," like the old Christian knights.

This book is an invitation to the reactionary cause. It's a declaration of war against "progress" and a call for peace with the natural order of things. It's a guide to happiness for humans living in a world where everything—government and business, pleasure and pain—has grown to an inhuman scale.

So, let's begin.

PART I

That Was Then

CHAPTER ONE

The Reactionary's Dreams of Heaven

Life in the Middle Ages was not a nightmare, but a dream—an amorous dream of heaven.
—Ramiro de Maeztu

I magine a land where the average citizen lives on about twelve acres of land, and the poorest of the poor get by with just one. None of them have ever seen the road darkened by a skyscraper or heard the air split by the sound of a passing airplane. Nearly 100 percent of the population lives and works in the great outdoors. Their skin is a healthy bronze; their hands are strong and calloused; their muscles are hard, taut, and eminently practical, earned through long days of wholesome labor.

There are no pesticides or growth hormones in this country. All the meat and vegetables they eat are totally organic. Their furniture is what we would call antique, fashioned by master craftsmen in the local style and passed down from father to son over generations. To heat their homes, they burn wood in the fireplace. Of course, they chop the wood themselves.

Here, nothing is disposable—and nothing need be. When a man's trouser catches a nail, his wife can darn the tear in a matter of minutes.

In fact, she herself made the trousers from wool her husband sheared from his own sheep. If a chair breaks, her husband fells a tree and carves a new one. Tinkering at these pleasant little chores under the shade of an oak tree might even be a definition of happiness.

For the most part, these folks walk everywhere they need to go. It keeps them fit and limber. Besides, they're never far from town: everything they need is, at most, a few miles from the front door. Not one of them has ever seen a throughway or a byway, and no tractor trailer has ever disturbed the quiet of this little domain. The only sounds a man hears are the whistle of the scythe as his son mows the barley, the low of the heifer as she brushes away flies with her tail, and the voice of his wife calling him in for lunch.

Of course, the routine changes slightly as the year goes on. Life here is tied to the seasons.

In spring, the men stay up all night drinking craft beer, roasting pigs and lambs for the Easter feast. This they'll eat with apples and plums and wild strawberries. The boys will crown the girls with garlands of wildflowers and woo them with memorized poetry. Broods of children will chase rabbits through the briar. Someone will play the guitar and the people will dance.

Come autumn, the men will hunt deer and geese. The harvest feast will be marked with hearty vegetable stews, tart cider or warm brandy, and all sorts of homemade cheeses. The men will build a great bonfire; the people will sing and dance; and when the celebration ends, families will walk home to their cottages. There's perfect silence over the valley. An owl hoots somewhere deep in the forest; a badger chitters in the brush.

Here, there are no streetlamps or strip malls. Once the sun sets, all is dark. Every living thing looks up and sees the same pale moon looming amid a crowd of stars. The road ahead is lit by these heavenly bodies. How could it be otherwise?

Welcome to a day in the life of a serf.

That's a slightly romanticized view...but only slightly. Our view of the Middle Ages has been clouded by centuries of bad history piled on top of one another. So, before we go any further, we must clear up three common misconceptions about our friend the serf.

1. The serf was oppressed.

The defining characteristic of serfdom, it would seem, is a total lack of freedom. But what do we mean by *freedom*? Usually, we mean exactly what the Marquis de Sade would mean: the ability to exercise one's agency to fulfill one's desire. The modern would probably say freedom is the ability to "live your best life."

Freedom, then, is about choices. The more our choices align with our desire, the freer we think ourselves to be. For instance, the citizen of a communist country gets his bread by standing in a bread line. Everyone receives the same crusty loaf with the same bland wrapper. They have no choice; they are not free. The citizen of a capitalist country, meanwhile, goes to the grocery store. Does he want Wonder Bread, Pepperidge Farm, Nature's Own, Sara Lee, Arnold, or store brand? Does he prefer white? Wheat? Rye? Pumpernickel? Cinnamon raisin? Sprouted grain? Gluten free? He has choices; he is free.

Theoretically, this should mean that the man who shops at the largest store is the freest. That's what we mean when we say that a store has the "best selection" in town: that it has the most *options* to choose from.

But if freedom is defined as the ability to choose from as many options as possible, then freedom is automatically defined by income. In theory, I can walk to Market Basket and choose from hundreds of different breads, the cheapest of which costs $1.99. Yet, if I have only two dollars in my pocket, I have only one choice, which is really no choice at all. If I have only one dollar in my pocket, then I have less "freedom" than our comrade in the breadline, who at least gets some bread.

This isn't an apologetic for communism, of course. But maybe we can see how our definition of freedom is a bit muddled.

What's more, chains like Trader Joe's and ALDI are quickly building a supermarket empire by taking *away* choice. They realized that Americans like choice in theory but hate it in practice. We're highly susceptible to option paralysis. While we'd be perfectly content eating any of the hundreds of breads in the baked goods aisle, having to pick just one causes us mental anguish. We're actually glad when someone makes such decisions for us.

This is the case with so much of modern America. We have more choices than we have desires. In fact, there's a whole segment of the economy devoted to *creating* desire for products that already exist but that nobody ever wanted. It's called advertising. In a sane economy, supply responds to demand. In America's capitalist economy, we create the supply and then manufacture the demand. Nobody wanted a Chia Pet or an iPhone until someone offered to sell it to him for a reasonable price. Anyway, what's a "reasonable price" for something you don't want and don't need?

So we can't say that the serf was oppressed merely because he lacked choices. In fact, I would argue that he was *freer*, because he was free from meaningless choices. If he wanted bread, he baked it.

And this goes well beyond economics. We feel not only entitled to our infinite choices but obligated to make them with the utmost care. There are eight billion people on earth, and we have to find the perfect one to marry. There are more than twenty-six thousand colleges on the planet, and we have to attend the one that's just the right fit for us. Then we have to move to our ideal city and land our dream job, which will allow us to buy our dream car and go on our dream vacation to an island paradise in the Caribbean. If we don't, we'll die unhappy and unfulfilled.

This is nonsense, of course, but many Americans think this way, even if unconsciously, and it's making us miserable. We are always free to choose, but never free from choice. We lack the greatest freedom of all: freedom from desire, otherwise known as gratitude.

Chesterton once said that "thanks is the highest form of thought, and gratitude is happiness doubled by wonder." This has always been the position taken by the Catholic Church. Christian serfs were warned against greed and urged to thank God for what little they had. Most of our contemporaries would probably call that a form of propaganda meant to defend the lairds from their envious peasants. Well, the American middle class enjoys prosperity beyond anything the fattest, richest laird in all the Middle Ages could have dreamt of. We have infinitely more to be grateful for, and yet we're infinitely less grateful for it.

Gratitude for the blessings of his life is what made the serf's lot such a happy one. He lived his whole life in the village where he was born. He began apprenticing for the family business as soon as he was old enough to hold a shovel or carry a hammer. He married some girl he'd known and befriended since childhood. He was baptized, confirmed, married, and buried in the same church he attended every Sunday. In other words, he was blissfully free of all the basically meaningless choices that we moderns spend the first fifty years of our lives agonizing over. By the time he was eighteen, he could get on with *living*.

2. The serf was ignorant.

When we picture a serf in our mind's eye, we see an illiterate, superstitious bigot, his boots caked with manure and his face full of warts. He couldn't read; he couldn't vote. If he wanted music, he had to sing it himself. If he wanted art, he had to content himself with the statues in his parish church. He was uncultured and uncouth—trapped in a religious-political system in which he had no say, and which he couldn't understand even if he did.

How unlike us moderns! We spend our days reading Plato and listening to Beethoven. For long hours we wander through museums, or else simply plant ourselves beneath an oak tree and contemplate the unity of all Creation. On Fridays, we gather with our friends for our weekly symposia; we drink wine and discuss Confucius and Augustine and al-Ghazali. And we're all very proud of those wise, benevolent elected officials we send to Washington.

It's amusing to consider how many wars were fought to empty a little scripture out of the peasant's head and fill it with a bunch of sitcoms and pornography. It's doubly amusing to read the accounts of men who thought the future might develop otherwise. The *philosophes* believed the Revolution would bring about a grand Republic of Letters, governed by a mass of learned and virtuous citizens guided by pure reason. Friedrich Engels believed that, in a communist society, the proletariat would become like his bourgeois friends: they would drink champagne, eat caviar, and foxhunt.

It never occurred to these men that most people might not *want* to be lettered. They might not have much interest in the fancy things afforded by Herr Engels's trust fund.

To be fair, this isn't a uniquely modern error. It has its origins at the very beginning of philosophy. In the first line of his *Metaphysics*, Aristotle declares, "All men by nature desire to know." It's a nice sentiment, but a false one. Let me prove it to you.

In your pocket, there's a little black box. Using that little black box, you can read every known work of Seneca, Euclid, Xenophon, Aquinas, Pascal, Shakespeare, Milton, Montaigne, Donne, Johnson, and Dickens. But you probably won't. You'll use it to look at pictures of strange-looking cats and watch videos of men hitting each other in the groin. And that's not your fault! Human beings, on the main, simply aren't very curious.

This is the confounding thing about the Enlightenment. It's true that all men are, to some degree, rational. But it's also true that all men are, to some degree, creative. We are all, to some degree, funny. Why on earth should we single out *reason* as the basis of our society? The idea of a "Republic of Letters" is only slightly less ridiculous than that of a Republic of Paintings or a Republic of Comedies.

I say "slightly less" because every human being possesses a rational soul. We are defined by reason in a way we aren't defined by creativity or humor. But assuming that men will make good use of their rational souls was a pretty big gamble and, so far, it hasn't paid off.

That's the trouble with our political, economic, and cultural institutions. They were devised by men who, like Aristotle, believed that every man could be a philosopher and assumed that every man wanted to be one. The feudal order was built on the opposite assumption. The medievals assumed that most men didn't want to be philosophers: they were content to be men.

3. The serf was miserable.

I suppose, if we went back in time, we could poll a few thousand serfs and find out what percent of them were miserable. Then we could compare that data to modern statistics. That would settle the question definitively.

How are we doing in twenty-first-century America? According to the Centers for Disease Control and Prevention, about 10 percent of Americans have medical records that list them as clinically depressed. In 2017, a Harris poll reported that 72 percent of Americans feel persistently lonely. In 2019, YouGov found that one in five millennials claim to have no friends at all.

It's hard to believe that our peasant friends would have worse numbers.

Many conservatives would balk at the idea of judging our social order based on happiness, but every question about humanity must concern itself with happiness; it's the whole reason for our existence.

This is one of the fundamental truths of the Christian religion. The *Baltimore Catechism*, in its sweet and simple way, puts it thus:

> Q. Why did God make you?
> A. God made me to know Him, to love Him, and to serve Him in this world, and to be happy with Him forever in heaven.

Now, that last clause is certainly important. Trying to make everyone as happy on earth as in heaven is to *immanentize the eschaton*, as conservative highbrows like to say. It's the very essence of utopian thinking, and the reactionary is even more allergic to utopianism than the conservative.

Yet the fact remains that humans are meant for happiness, in a deep and metaphysical sense. Men are made to be happy. The founding fathers understood this and had the wisdom to enshrine "the pursuit of happiness" on our republic's birth certificate.

Back when he was a conservative, the columnist George F. Will wrote a book called *The Pursuit of Virtue and Other Tory Notions*. Yet Mr. Will missed the point, perhaps because he's an atheist. The pursuit of happiness is the Toriest notion of all.

Virtue is certainly a necessary aspect of human happiness. A man can't really be happy as he wallows in sin. Whatever debased pleasure he might feel, it's not worthy of the name happiness.

The pursuit of happiness was at the center of the medieval worldview. They understood (as every Christian does) that we cannot be happy without God—that God *is* our happiness. "Our hearts are restless, Lord, until they rest in thee," as Saint Augustine said. There's no better word for the condition of modern man: restless. He is oppressed by his own false freedom, tortured by his inflamed appetites, and humiliated by his own ignorance. The things that might make him truly happy—gratitude and simplicity, peace and quiet— are kept forever out of his reach.

Whatever else we want to say about the Middle Ages, that certainly wasn't true of the happy serf, whose gratitude and simplicity were a matter of faith and routine. Such happiness was not only independent of wealth, but it could be found *in* poverty; gratitude was something that could be felt *even after the collapse of a civilization.* Saint Augustine witnessed firsthand the fall of the Roman Empire, the event that inaugurated the so-called Dark Ages, otherwise known as the early Middle Ages. This was a turning point in the history of Christianity. As Charles Van Doren (himself no reactionary) wrote, "Where wealth had been the measure of a Roman, now poverty became the measure of a Christian."

It was poverty, yes. Specifically, it was Lady Poverty: the maiden in the desert who won the heart of that great chevalier, Saint Francis of Assisi. In his blessed poverty, the medieval man found a reflection of Christ himself, the poor carpenter's Son and the source of all true happiness. As Van Doren observed, "The Christian of the Dark Ages also felt that the greatest of human pleasures was to praise the Creator. . . . Simple meals, a simple life, time to contemplate eternity, and a voice free to praise God—what more could man want?"

We cannot remake the world as twelfth-century France, but what we can do is recognize that a happy society would look much more like twelfth-century France than twenty-first-century America. If one believes with Louis de Bonald that Christianity is "but the application to society of every moral truth," then one would want our society to be in some meaningful way Christian. In the Middle Ages we have the singular example of a purely Christian society. It was isolated from the old paganism by the yawning Dark Ages and not yet spoiled by paganism's return in the fifteenth century.

If we are ever to re-Christianize the West, the result will *necessarily* look like the Middle Ages—and for the reactionary, that is a happy outcome, because he knows, better than anyone, that the worship of progress is the worship of a false god. But before we can reclaim what we've lost, including our easy access to happiness, we must humiliate our pride, our idolization of progress, and give a fair hearing to the ages and the peoples that have gone before us.

CHAPTER TWO

The Reactionary's Code: Loyal and Joyful

Brute beauty and valour and act, oh, air,
pride, plume, here
Buckle! And the fire that breaks from thee then,
a billion
Times told lovelier, more dangerous, O my
chevalier!

—Gerard Manley Hopkins

The serfs, we know, were the low rung of feudal society. What we might not remember is that the feudalism of the Middle Ages lasted for a *thousand years*—and that was *not* because kings and nobles demanded it, knights enforced it, and serfs cowered before an all-powerful clergy who justified it and sanctified it. This modern view of the Middle Ages is fundamentally wrong, Marxist, and ridiculous. Feudalism—as an economic, political, religious, and cultural order—survived for so long because people *believed* in it; they believed in its values of faithfulness, service, charity, honor, duty, sacrifice, and, most of all, chivalry. They fell short of these values, they fought over them, but they always labored to restore them.

The noblemen of the Middle Ages were more than high-born or well-bred. They were supposed to be chivalrous—from the French *chevalier*, meaning horseman, or knight. Properly understood, the nobility were the knights—men worthy of riding a horse. This was the great measure of the medieval man. For "knights have not been chosen to ride an ass or a mule," as Díaz de Gámez, a chronicler of knighthood, notes. "They have not been taken from among feeble or timid or cowardly souls, but from among who are strong and full of energy, bold and without fear; and so there is no other beast that so befits a knight as a good horse."

Such strong, energetic, bold, and fearless men were the upholders of the way of life known as chivalry, which was the standard by which *every* man in the Middle Ages—serf or knight, priest or lord or king—held himself. One scholar has called chivalry a medieval "framework for lay society." It wasn't a code of conduct so much as a spirituality—the only comprehensive spirituality for Christians (besides priests and monks) in history.

Its origins are to be found in the very establishment of medieval society. For the first few centuries *anno Domini*, Christians existed as a persecuted sect. Even after the faith became the official religion of the Roman Empire, the "framework" of society was still Roman. That changed after the Fall of Rome and the disappearance of the Pax Romana. From this apparent calamity, Christians took the opportunity to create a civilization in their own image—fully aware that Christ's kingdom is not of this world, which belongs to the devil (John 14:30).

C. S. Lewis put it better than anyone, perhaps. "Enemy-occupied territory," he wrote, "that is what this world is. Christianity is the story of how the rightful king has landed, you might say landed in disguise, and is calling us to take part in a great campaign of sabotage."

And so, in the Middle Ages, life itself became a crusade, not against heathens and Mussulmen, but against the devil. The worthy man waged an endless war against sin and, to the extent that he was sinful, himself. In that sense, a good Christian is a noble Christian, and every Christian was, and is, a knight.

A knight, like a monk, is an ascetic of sorts. The great chivalric authors rail against vanity and wantonness. Geoffroi de Charny writes of knights, "[W]hen it is cold, they endure the cold, and when it is hot, they put up with the heat." They don't waste any time lounging in "white sheets and soft beds," for "the longer you sleep, the less time you will have to acquire knowledge and to learn something of value." They certainly don't play "ball games," which are a "woman's pastime and pleasure." (He meant tennis.) And they are neither gourmets nor gourmands. "Do not concern yourself with being knowledgeable about good dishes and fine sauces nor spend too much time deciding which wines are the best," Sir Geoffroi advises, "and you will live more at ease." He recommends that a knight who succumbs to these appetitive hobbies "should have all his teeth put out."

Nor is a good knight a snob. He knows that the worthiest men are seldom the richest. "You should not care about amassing great wealth," Sir Geoffroi warns, "for the more worldly goods a man acquires, the more reluctant he is to die and the greater his fear of death." He continues, "Do not despise poor men or those of lesser rank than you, for there are many poor men who are of greater worth than the rich." Besides, every true knight knows "impoverished fighting companions who are sometimes worth as much or more than some great lord."

The code of chivalry held that the bravest and most gallant warriors should also be the meekest and gentlest men. Sir Geoffroi wrote that knights ought to be "humble among their friends, proud and bold against their foes, tender and merciful towards those who need assistance, cruel avengers against their enemies," and "pleasant and amiable with all others."

Knights should be self-deprecating. "Speak of the achievements of others, but not of yourself," says Sir Geoffroi, for "where there is arrogance, there reigns anger and all kinds of folly; and where humility is to be found, there reigns good sense and happiness." Knights also appreciate the value of silence. Our Blessed Lord once declared, "I tell you, on the day of judgment men will render account for every careless word they utter." So, Sir Geoffroi informs us, the knight will "take care not to talk too much, for in talking too much you are sure to say something foolish; for example, the foolish cannot hold their peace, and the wise know how to hold their peace until it is time to speak."

What do knights enjoy, then? They like hardship, challenge, and exertion—becoming stronger in mind, body, and soul. "Because of their great desire to reach and attain that high honor," writes Sir Geoffroi, "they do not care what sufferings they have to endure, but turn everything into great enjoyment." For "strength of purpose and cheerfulness of heart makes it possible to bear all these things gladly and confidently." Knights, to this end, "should never tire of engaging in the pastimes of jousting, conversation, dancing, and singing in the company of ladies and damsels." Indeed, "the best pastime of all is to be often in good company."

As chivalry developed, and the memory of paganism faded, knights prayed to be as chaste as they were courageous. In the later Arthurian cycles, for instance, Sir Perceval is told, "[H]ad your body been violated by the corruption of sin, you would have forfeited your primacy among the Companions of the Quest" for the Holy Grail.

Remember, too, the famed affair between Launcelot and Guinevere, which causes a civil war in Britain and the death of King Arthur himself. Wracked by guilt, Guinevere retreats into a convent, and Launcelot to a hermitage, later to be ordained a priest. They don't meet again in this life. Warned in a dream that she is about to die,

Guinevere prays that she may never see her lover again. Launcelot arrives at her nunnery half an hour after she expires. As Sir Thomas Malory writes, "[H]e wept not greatly, but sighed. And so he did all the observance of the service himself, both the dirige, and on the morn he sang mass."

This is how the greatest courtly romance ends: not in amours, or even tears, but in sackcloth and ashes and penance and sighs.

Launcelot dies of his sorrow not long after. Yet he's remembered not as a villain, but as a hero—a valiant warrior, a sinner who atoned for his sins. Laying him to rest, Sir Ector says of his dead comrade Launcelot:

> And thou were the courteoust knight that ever bare shield. And thou were the truest friend to thy lover that ever bestrad horse. And thou were the truest lover of a sinful man that ever loved woman. And thou were the kindest man that ever struck with sword. And thou were the goodliest person that ever came among press of knights. And thou was the meekest man and the gentlest that ever ate in hall among ladies. And thou were the sternest knight to thy mortal foe that ever put spear in the rest.

When Sir Ector finishes his speech, Malory writes, "there was weeping and dolor out of measure" among the Round Table.

All in all, though, knights were happy warriors. As Sir Geoffroi notes, they took pleasure in "glances and desire, love, reflection, and memory, gaiety of heart and liveliness of body."

Above all, however, a knight was a servant of Holy Mother Church. This was the knight's great cause and his first loyalty. It required of him strength, courage, and martial training. "To preserve and maintain the rights of the Holy Church," Sir Geoffroi writes, "one should not hold back from committing oneself to their defense by war and battle, if they cannot be maintained in any other way."

While a fighting man, the knight remains pious. Ramon Llull says that "it is the office of the knight to uphold and defend the Holy Catholic Faith." Therefore, "the greatest friendship there can be in this world should be between cleric and knight," and "the knight is not upholding the Order of Chivalry if he contravenes and disobeys the clerics who are obliged to love and uphold the Order and Chivalry." Indeed, "he who neither loves nor fears God is not worthy of joining the order."

As a Christian, the knight was expected to take special care of the indigent and outcast. "It is the office of the knight to support widows, orphans, and the helpless," Llull writes, "just as it is customary and right that the mighty help to defend the weak, and the weak to take refuge in the strong."

A knight should be magnanimous; knighthood is about service, not profit. "You should never regret any generosity you may show and any gifts well bestowed," Sir Geoffroi assures us. "Above all," he warns, "refrain from enriching yourself at others' expense, especially from the limited resources of the poor, for unsullied poverty is worth more than corrupt wealth."

The goal was not to die rich. It was not to profit from others. It was not to pursue one's own goals or desires or choices. No, the medieval goal was something quite different. It was to live, as Sir Geoffroi summed it up, "loyally and joyfully." Friendship and happiness, service and charity, courage and compassion were the goals of the chivalrous man. That was the medieval ideal. And it is the reactionary's ideal as well. The modern world offers nothing better.

CHAPTER THREE

Why the Reactionary Has a Sneaking Suspicion for Savonarola

Life is so full of meaning and purpose, so full of beauty… that you will find earth but cloaks your heaven.

—Girolamo Savonarola

What should strike us about the Middle Ages is not how hierarchical it was, but how egalitarian it was. It wasn't egalitarian in the radical sense: the banker's son and the farmer's daughter standing in the same breadline, or the noblest duke and the humblest vicar marching to the same guillotine. But there was the natural equality of a society ordered on the idea that all men and women are children of God. The poor were not to envy the rich, the rich were admonished to remember their duty to the poor, and kings rode into battle with their knights.

In the Middle Ages, all men, regardless of their station, enjoyed the same pastimes: hunting, fishing, wrestling, dancing, singing, and drinking. In fact, the code of chivalry required that the higher a man's station, the manlier he be. If the liege lost an arm-wrestling contest, he might also lose his authority.

No popular, manly interest was scorned by the elite; by the same token, no fine art was dismissed by common folks as elitist. Lords and serfs listened to the same troubadours and watched the same jugglers. They heard the same epics recited by the same bards. They told their children the same tales about giants and wizards and the Lady in the Lake. They crowded together in the streets to watch the same plays put on by the same amateur troupes composed of local butchers and bakers. A good joust or a public execution was enjoyed by all.

It's impossible to understand medieval culture without bearing in mind that it was, everywhere and always, a form of entertainment. It was stuff that people *liked*, without any airs or pretensions. The word "culture" itself has, in our own time, become identical with "high culture"—that is, stuff people pretend to like because it makes them feel smart.

Much of medieval culture was devotional. Hundreds of people would gather in the center of town to watch a mystery play. The three bestselling books of the age were the Bible, *The Imitation of Christ* by Thomas à Kempis, and *The Consolation of Philosophy* by the martyr Boethius. But most of the literature was, literally, epic. Like *The Canterbury Tales*, *The Knight of the Grail*, and the *Poem of the Cid*, they were stories of gallant knights, saucy monks, and ugly women who become beautiful women with the breaking of a curse. Sir Thomas Malory's *Le Morte d'Arthur* is the most exciting and compelling book in history; it's also incredibly repetitive and almost childishly simplistic. It reads like the transcript of a father's bedtime story to his son, because it probably was, originally. The oral tradition of storytelling was so strong, and literacy so uncommon, that most medieval texts—even nonfiction works, like Geoffroi de Charny's *Book of Chivalry*—are almost impossible to follow unless one is a little tipsy and reading aloud.

What comes through in medieval literature is a civilization built on high Christian ideals, animated by chivalry, held across every social stratum. But chivalry and medieval egalitarianism faded into the Renaissance. Medieval society centered around the Church became Renaissance society centered around man and distinctions among men. Thus, the fancy and the pretentious displaced the simple and the humble. Men thought less of Christian brotherhood and more about social status.

As scholars such as Régine Pernoud have shown definitively, the conventional history of the Renaissance is total bunk. There was no "rediscovery" of classical texts in the West after the fall of Byzantium. Plato, Aristotle, Cicero, and other great classical authors were read and quoted widely by literate medievals—one need only remember Thomas Aquinas, the greatest Aristotelian since Aristotle.

The Renaissance was not the moment Europe emerged from darkness, but the hour it descended into mania, an all-encompassing obsession with antiquity that swept the educated classes, reshaping philosophy, theology, architecture, poetry, theatre, sculpture, and even baby names. As such, the Renaissance created a fissure between the people and the elite, as the appreciation of such "culture" required education. Really, it was posturing and pretension, little different from the posturing and pretension we see among our educated elites today, who separate the world into the respectable educated classes like themselves and the uneducated deplorables who might disagree with them.

The Renaissance was subversive by its very nature, asserting the culture of the pagan, classical world *against* the medieval Christian order. The question, then, is: *Why* this revolt against the Middle Ages?

Those who launched and perpetuated the Renaissance found the medieval worldview bleak, pessimistic, and limiting. If life was nothing but a vale of tears, and man himself merely a sinner, then no real happiness could be found in this world, and all we could do was submit to the authorities, say our prayers, and hope we make it to heaven.

Of course, the medieval worldview wasn't gloomy pessimism, but hard-nosed realism; man *is* a sinner. To a Christian, that's just reality, and denying it denies a truth about human nature. The Renaissance men weren't humanists, but anti-humanists who misdirected people's desire for happiness away from God, where it belongs, to social and intellectual distinction, where, at best, it can be found only in part.

The Renaissance ideal was also hopelessly shallow. We can see this in Renaissance art—something in which men of the Renaissance took great pride. I won't deny that the *Venus of Urbino* is attractive. I'm sure Titian's model turned a few heads in sixteenth-century Venice. But ask a forty-year-old man who the most beautiful woman in the world is. If he describes a sixteen-year-old girl with milky skin and curly golden hair, we'd probably call him a pervert. We certainly wouldn't call him a humanist.

Everyone knows what beauty is, in the most prosaic sense— attractiveness, or being pleasant to look at. Why, then, pay the admission at a museum just to see paintings of beautiful women when you can find the real thing at every market, café, and restaurant on the planet? The point of art is to capture a deeper beauty than the merely sensual.

The contrast between the medieval and the Renaissance view is most pronounced, for obvious reasons, in religious art.

Judging by the Shroud of Turin, Our Lord was a very good-looking man. Yet none of the Gospel writers felt the need to say so. Not one of them recalls women swooning as they listened to his sermons. And why should they have? Jesus's appearance is irrelevant. The point is that he appeared.

The medievals would have found the Renaissance obsession with making Christ as attractive as possible absurd. It was trivializing, almost blasphemous, as if we might as well have followed Barabbas had he thicker hair or a stronger jawline. The medieval artistic challenge was to bring all of Jesus's aspects into visible harmony. How does one depict the King of the Universe enthroned in glory, bearing in mind that he was born in a barn and worked most of his life as a carpenter? How can a single face be at once meek and mighty, gentle and terrible, full of kindness and full of wrath? That is, technically, the more pious preoccupation. It's also vastly more interesting and demands of the artist a much rarer skill and depth of understanding.[1]

Compare Titian's *Venus of Urbino* to Botticelli's *The Birth of Venus*. Erik von Kuehnelt-Leddihn rightly called the latter a "baptized Venus," "surrounded by a hardly perceptible glow of sensuality, yet expressing a real synthesis of Eros and Agape, earthly and divine love." She's nude, yes, but her face is kind. Her eyes shine with a sort of innocent curiosity. There's nothing of the haughty, cruel, alluring gaze of the *Urbino*.

How do we explain the difference? Botticelli was a disciple of Fra Girolamo Savonarola, the great Florentine reformer. No doubt you learned in school that Savonarola was a fanatical friar who drove the Medicis—those great patrons of art—out of Florence. Then he took all the art and books in the city, heaped them in a pile, and lit a match. His was the original "bonfire of the vanities." Like almost everything else we think we know about the Renaissance, this is a lie.

Savonarola loved good art, certainly enough to hate bad art. And, in those days, there was a lot of bad art, much of it patronized by the Medicis, who were great patrons of art in the sense that they were incredibly rich and gave money to almost every artist in the city. The fact that they chose popular tunes and repurposed them for court prayers should be enough to tell you that it's purely by chance that they managed to patronize anything of worth. The fact that

Michelangelo, Botticelli, and Pico della Mirandola (along with dozens of other artists we now consider Renaissance masters) were devoted followers of Savonarola should tell you something about him and his artistic tastes.

Savonarola won the devotion of these geniuses by simply restating the medieval view of art. As he declared in one sermon:

> Beauty is transfiguration, it is light. Essential beauty, in its perfection, must therefore be looked for beyond the sphere of visible objects.... The more creatures approach and participate in the beauty of God, the more are they themselves beautiful, just as the beauty of the body is in proportion to the beauty of the soul. For, if you were to take two women of this audience, equally beautiful in body, it would be the holier one that would excite the most admiration amongst the beholders, and the palm would assuredly be given to her even by worldly men.

The crowds who heard his homilies would have been familiar with the works of history's greatest Florentine, Dante Alighieri. Dante rarely spoke of his beloved Beatrice's outer beauty. It was her great virtue, her kindness, her modesty that possessed him. So he began his finest love poem:

> My lady looks so gentle and so pure,
> When yielding salutation by the way,
> That the tongue trembles and has naught to say,
> And the eyes, which fain would see, may not endure.

The city's most brilliant artists heeded Savonarola's strictures. They wanted their paintings to be beautiful, not merely voluptuous.

They wanted to create art, not pornography. And how should they do it? Savonarola gave this advice: "Recollect the story of David going forth against the giant Goliath. Let alone that clumsy armor of logic and philosophy, and arm thyself with a lively and simple faith, after the example of the apostles and the martyrs."

The friar wasn't opposed to classical writers any more than his fellow Dominican, and great Aristotelian, Thomas Aquinas was. He encouraged the study of Homer, Virgil, Cicero, Plato, and Aristotle. But not at the expense of the plain, simple truths of the Bible.

Savonarola believed that beautiful art arises from beautiful hearts, hearts that "participate in the beauty of God." How does a painter participate in that beauty except by practicing the Christian faith? How can one hope to depict all of Christ's aspects in harmony without meeting him first in scripture, at the Mass, and in prayer?

Savonarola's adherents were so ashamed of their earlier works that they willingly consigned their own "vanities" to the friar's bonfires.

Alas, one friar could only do so much. After Savonarola was martyred in 1498, the Renaissance succumbed to its pagan, classicist temptations. Less than one hundred years after Savonarola's death came the advent of the baroque, an effete, garish, cloyingly sensual movement in Western art. Nothing could have been further from the common tastes of simple, ordinary medieval men. Caravaggio, for instance, made Jesus Christ and Saint Francis look soft and languid, male prostitutes rather than martyrs. When it comes to painting and sculpture, it has all been downhill since Savonarola's bonfires were doused. Things have gotten far worse than Fra Girolamo could have imagined.

Piss Christ (1987) by Andres Serrano, a crucifix floating in a jar of urine, is conservatives' go-to example for blasphemous, "edgy" modern art. Yet Mr. Serrano insists that he meant no offense. "I've been a Catholic all my life," he told a reporter. He claims he was only trying to capture the gruesomeness of the crucifixion, which has been sanitized by traditional religious art. "Maybe if Piss Christ upsets you," Mr. Serrano continues, "it's because it gives some sense of what the crucifixion was actually like."

Conservative critics rightly observe that Our Lord didn't die in a vat of bodily fluids, but Mr. Serrano's stated aim was similar to Mel Gibson's in making his 2004 blockbuster *The Passion of the Christ*. Mr. Gibson told an interviewer, "I wanted it to be shocking," so that the audience could see the "extreme pain and suffering and ridicule" that Jesus endured on our behalf.

Again, this misses the point, not only of the Crucifixion, but of art itself. Would Christ's sacrifice have been more meaningful if he'd suffered more? If, for instance, he stayed on the cross for three days instead of a couple of hours? Or what if the authorities had tortured him more before sending him to die—pulled out his teeth, ripped out his fingernails, slit the soles of his feet before marching him to Calvary? Hell: the thieves who were crucified alongside Christ had their shins broken by the legionaries. Should we worship them instead because they perhaps suffered more?

The point isn't that a Jewish preacher died a horrible death in or around the year AD 33. The point is that he was the Son of God, the Word Incarnate. He spent his earthly life healing the sick, raising the dead, casting out demons, and teaching men the way to paradise. He deserves to be worshipped, adored, and glorified; instead, when he was on this earth, he was stripped, beaten, and executed. This is what medieval art tried to capture: not the goriness of the death, but the purity of the victim.

For those who don't realize that Jesus is the Christ, he's just another victim of the Roman legal system. For those who do, a little blood on his palms and a little hole by his heart tell us all we need to know. As that poor genius Peter Abelard wrote four hundred years before Savonarola:

> For they are ours, O Lord, our deeds, our deeds,
> Why must Thou suffer torture for our sins?
> Let our hearts suffer for Thy passion, Lord,
> That sheer compassion may Thy mercy win.

For the Christian, that's enough.

One biographer wrote that Savonarola "sought to exorcise science and the arts possessed with the demon of Paganism. It was in the name of the prophets who had cried woe to whomsoever should bow the knee to idols."

The Renaissance idolized man, and it set the stage for another, more successful attempt to replace medieval Christendom. This time the challenge came not from paganism, but from Protestantism, which led men down a different, but also perilous, path. Ironically, the Reformation began explicitly as a rejection of the Renaissance re-paganization of society, with Martin Luther going so far as to call Aristotle's *Ethics* "the worst enemy of grace." But while the universities' turn away from the Bible towards classical philosophy might have been a regressive act, it was Protestantism, as a political movement, that finally broke Christendom.

CHAPTER FOUR

Why Reactionaries Defend the Inquisition

It is absurd to argue men, as to torture them,
into believing.
—John Henry Newman

I n 2018, the U.S. Conference of Catholic Bishops named Sir
Thomas More and Bishop John Fisher as patron saints for their
"Religious Freedom Week." More is, without a doubt, one of history's most interesting men. England's greatest humanist, he was celebrated as a politician, author, lawyer, and scholar. He was also a pioneer of investment banking and a gifted astronomer. All in all, he's a fine patron for any endeavor.

I couldn't help but chuckle, however, at the bishops' choice, because More was also a staunch defender of the Inquisition.

Fans of the HBO series *The Tudors* may know that. I assume most of *my* readers get their Henrician history from the 1966 film *A Man for All Seasons.* That movie helped to solidify More's reputation as a "martyr for conscience." It made him a humanist in the modern sense: a champion of gentle, liberal, forward-thinking values. More was many things—but not that.

A Man for All Seasons is one of my favorite movies, and it has some excellent set pieces, including the scene where the Duke of Norfolk begs Sir Thomas to join the English establishment, defy the pope, approve the annulment of the king's marriage to Catherine, and celebrate his marriage to Anne Boleyn. Their conversation goes like this:

> *Norfolk*: Oh, confound all this. I'm not a scholar. I don't know whether the marriage was lawful or not. But, damn it, Thomas, look at these names! Why can't you do as I did and come with us, for fellowship?
>
> *More*: And when we die, and you are sent to heaven for doing your conscience, and I am sent to hell for not doing mine, will you come with me—for fellowship?

Catholics (and especially English Catholics) have always proclaimed the indissolubility of conscience. Cardinal Newman called it "a magisterial dictate" and "the aboriginal Vicar of Christ." Hence his famous toast: "If I am obliged to bring religion into after-dinner toasts, I shall drink to Conscience first, and to the Pope afterwards."

Nevertheless, More also wrote that "the burning of heretics" is "lawful, necessary, and well done"—a "good and politic provision of the temporality." By "temporality" he meant *government*, and that was the crux of his argument.

Contrary to popular history, the Catholic Church didn't indiscriminately burn every heretic it found. In fact, the Church never burned heretics at all. The Inquisition's job was to determine whether an individual was guilty of spreading heresy; the condemned was then turned over to the state for punishment. Few were punished with death—and it's those exceptions that we read about.

But, in fact, the Church constituted inquisitions only reluctantly—and, even then, the goal was often to protect heretics from zealous mobs, as was the case in 1211, when Peter Abelard appeared in Soissons to defend himself against charges of Sabellianism (a heresy involving the Trinity); the locals nearly stoned him to death.

The Church repeatedly intervened to prevent such theological vigilantism. Eventually, it did so through judicial (inquisitional) tribunals where heretics could testify in their own defense. The overwhelming majority of defendants were acquitted or had their sentences suspended. The Church, in defending its doctrine, also employed it, practicing charity. Most defendants were regarded as prodigal sons rather than hardened criminals. Many legal scholars claim the inquisitions were the first courts to systematically apply the principle of "innocent until proven guilty."

Still, defending heretics from angry mobs was one thing, but why would the state execute any heretics at all? Sir Thomas More wrote that the temporality made this provision "for the preservation, not of the faith only, but also of the peace among their people," because an outbreak of heresy could lead to civil unrest:

> And surely the princes be bounden that they shall not suffer their people by infidels to be invaded, so be they as deeply bounder that they shall not suffer their people to be seduced and corrupted by heretics, since the peril shall in short while grow to as great, both with men's souls withdrawn from God, and their goods lost, and their bodies destroyed by common sedition, insurrection, and open war, within the bowels of their own land.
>
> All of which may in the beginning be right easily avoided, by punishment of those few that be the first.

Which few well repressed, or if need so require, utterly
pulled up, there shall be far the fewer have lust to follow.

Sir Thomas More was a realist who understood that men really
aren't capable of "agreeing to disagree." In due course, conflicts
between rival sects will inevitably spill over into political tension,
violence in the streets, and perhaps even civil war.

But there was an even greater problem looming. What happens
when political leaders spread heresy (Protestantism) to advance
their own power? It was such a political movement which cost More
his life.

In 1521, Pope Leo X named King Henry VIII of England Fidei
Defensor (Defender of the Faith) for a tract he had co-written refut-
ing Martin Luther's sacramental theology. Henry was a convinced
and orthodox Catholic. It was only in 1534, after the pope refused to
annul Henry's marriage to Queen Catherine, that he created a new
"Church of England," naming himself supreme governor thereof. He
became the pope of his own little church, and his first order of business was to grant himself that annulment.

What followed were two enormously consequential develop-
ments. One was the dissolution of the monasteries and the end of
feudalism. Henry VIII's cronies resented the economic and political
power of the Catholic Church, which controlled about 30 percent of
England. When the king declared that his English church was independent of the Holy See, he had his excuse to seize about 70 percent
of the Church's land and distribute it among his favorites. It was a
patronage system to reward greedy squires—the so-called "New
Men"—with land and privilege if they would do the Crown's bidding.
English kings had deployed a similar strategy for generations to consolidate their power against the upper nobility, but under Henry, the
New Men had new ideas, Renaissance ideas, that harkened back to

Roman ideas of private property. While the noblest of England's nobility continued to honor their traditional duties to their serfs, many others had no such scruples. Not content simply to own the land and collect taxes from their peasants, they asserted their absolute right over the property. Peasants, whose families had peacefully worked and developed plots of land for a thousand years, suddenly found themselves reduced to mere sharecroppers. When the squires decided they could demand greater returns from the peasantry and sell land for a profit, it led to the return of a Roman-style, currency-based economy, and capital (money) replaced the feudum (fief; land) as the basis of wealth. Capitalism thus displaced feudalism as society's organizing economic principle. Some conservatives call this progress; the reactionary knows better.

The other development was a bloody, perpetual contest between Anglicans, Catholics, and the multiplying sects of Protestants. Henry's successor, Edward VI, persecuted Catholics. Edward's successor, Queen Mary, persecuted Protestants. Her successor, Elizabeth I, returned to persecuting Catholics. And so on. Their logic, whether they persecuted Catholics or Protestants, was to defend the peace and unity of the realm. As (the Anglican) Peter Hitchens once noted: "Elizabeth did not persecute Catholics for their religion. She punished those who actively engaged in treason against her, a wholly different thing."

With Elizabeth's death, the English throne passed to the House of Stuart. The Stuarts were Protestants with deep Catholic sympathies. Their reign saw the rise of a new religious sect—the Puritans—that posed a very different set of problems for the establishment.

The Puritans were Presbyterians and Congregationalists, meaning that—unlike Catholics and Anglicans—they rejected the office of bishop entirely. The first Stuart king of England, James I, realized that if a large portion of his subjects didn't believe that the bishops were divinely ordained authorities, it wouldn't be long before they concluded that the divine right of kings was also blasphemous. "No bishop, no king," he quipped. James was right, and the Puritans ended up killing his son, the good and holy Charles I. The Puritans' leader, Oliver Cromwell (great-nephew of Thomas Cromwell, Henry VIII's chief minister, whose family's wealth derived directly from the dissolution of the monasteries), abolished both the episcopacy and the monarchy. For six years, England was ruled as a Puritan theocracy. All this, let us remember, was a consequence of Henry's divorce from his wife Catherine.

Likewise, in Germany, political self-interest spread religious heresy. In the middle of the sixteenth century, several princes in northern Germany—led by Philip I of Hesse and John Frederick I of Saxony—adopted Lutheranism and allied with other Protestant princes against the political authority of Charles V, the Holy Roman Emperor, who retained the allegiance of southern Germany, Austria, and northern Italy.

Politics and religion were also conflated in France in its infamous "Wars of Religion" that pitted Waldensian and Calvinist Protestants against the Valois kings and their Catholic supporters. When the Valois king Henry III was assassinated, his rightful heir was his cousin Henry IV, king of Navarre (a small nation between France and Spain) and a Protestant. A powerful Catholic nobleman—Henry I, Duke of Guise—led the Catholic gentry in an uprising against the Navarrese claimant. The fighting ended when Henry IV famously declared "Paris is well worth a Mass" and converted to Catholicism.

France's Wars of Religion claimed upwards of four million lives. By contrast, to keep the peace in England, Chancellor Sir Thomas More ordered the execution of three heretics. So, which was the wiser course: maintaining the peace through the execution of three heretics, or resolving a political-religious dispute through war, four million dead, and one religious conversion? If you chose the former, you're in favor of the Inquisition; that was its point.

This isn't, however, a case for burning heretics today. There are too many of them now. But one thing remains constant—all societies must be based on a commonly held system of belief; and if the Catholic Church does not provide that system, something else will.

There is, however, one modern philosophy which asserts that civil order can be created without metaphysical claims. That philosophy is called liberalism, and it was brought to us, eventually, by Protestantism and capitalism, which overturned Christendom and the old feudal order. Liberalism acknowledges no political authority except that of the national legislature and the constitutions or laws that it ratifies.

The three great liberal revolutions of the seventeenth and eighteenth centuries all had religious aspects to them. The so-called "Glorious Revolution" in England was explicitly Protestant, the American Revolution involved colonies that had established churches, and the French Revolution waged war against the Catholic Church. Still, a certain breed of liberal will maintain that liberalism, secularism, and anticlericalism (or Protestantism) needn't go hand in hand. One excellent conservative journalist—Michael Brendan Dougherty of *National Review*—recently opined, "The argument for liberalism doesn't have to be based on a total liberal account of man's nature and destiny, but as a good-enough escape from the Wars of Religion."

This seems to have been the founding fathers' vision as well. They founded a republic whose laws were based on a basic, non-sectarian Christianity. John Adams confessed as much when he said, "Our Constitution was made only for a moral and religious people. It is wholly inadequate to the government of any other." That was a statement of fact, not an ideological opinion. The American government was founded by men steeped in a Christian culture, which is why it upheld what its founders considered God-given unalienable rights that would have made little sense to non-Christians.

Progressives, of course, will be quick to point out that the First Amendment declares: "Congress shall make no law respecting an establishment of religion...." And that's certainly true, though they often neglect to mention what follows: "or prohibiting the free exercise thereof." But the Constitution only applies to the federal government. The states—those thirteen little colonies which banded together to form the United States of America—had generous powers to impose religious dogmas on their citizens. Most of the original states had their own established churches. (In fact, New Hampshire only disestablished its state church after the Civil War.) The point of the Establishment Clause was to prevent the Congregationalist North from asserting itself over the Anglican South, and vice versa.

Some modern conservative philosophers (notably Patrick Deneen) have criticized the founding fathers for not doing enough to ensure the propagation of religion from one generation to the next. Yet John Adams also wrote the Massachusetts Constitution, in which he made his position abundantly clear:

> The happiness of a people, and the good order and preservation of civil government, essentially depend upon piety, religion and morality; and as these cannot be generally diffused through a community, but by the institution of the public worship of God, and of public instructions in piety, religion and morality: Therefore, to promote their happiness, and to secure the good order and preservation of their government, the people of this Commonwealth have a right to invest their Legislature with power to

authorize and require, and the Legislature shall, from time to time, authorize and require, the several towns, parishes, precincts, and other bodies politic, or religious societies, to make suitable provision at their own expense, for the institution of the public worship of God, and for the support and maintenance of public protestant teachers of piety, religion, and morality, in all cases, where such provision shall not be made voluntarily.

The founding fathers were not liberal secularists. On the contrary, they regarded Christianity as the natural and necessary support for their constitutional government; they merely left the duty of religious instruction to the adherents' respective churches and the various states. It was a design of federalism, not secularism.

Still, liberals raise a relevant point. Historically, Protestantism has shown a willingness to compromise with radicalism, helping Christian societies seamlessly transition to secularism without the violent upheavals that afflicted Catholic countries like France and Spain. For a reactionary, though, that observation is to Catholicism's credit. Nothing in history has disproven Cardinal Newman's claim that "[t]here is no medium, in true philosophy, between Atheism and Catholicity"—and if the reactionary's task is rebuilding a Christian society, it likely begins with reasserting the primacy of the Catholic Church in our lives. The choice, to vary Cardinal Newman slightly, might be Catholicism or socialism.

The Left—whether Antifa, Black Lives Matter, the Big Tech–media–academic–government complex, an increasingly radical Democratic Party—approaches politics with a kind of religious zeal, because it is replacing the old common metaphysic, the Christian one, with a new one. Liberalism, which claimed that civil order can be created without metaphysical claims, has, for the most part, become leftism, which goes under the heading of social Marxism or "wokeism."

The new leftists have their own strange gnostic theories that deny material reality; they believe that a biological man may, in some awesome and transcendent way, be a woman. They believe that being a white heterosexual man is a sign, like the mark of Cain, that one is inherently and irredeemably evil. Where Christians blame original sin for all the evils of the world, the new leftists blame white people and capitalism (a product of white people). They have their own inquisitions, which enforce the dogmas of political correctness. They have their own witch hunts, which sniff out dissenters from their ideology and hound them out of government, corporations, and universities.[1]

The fact is, far-left political factions have always—*always*—evolved into secular religions. The Jacobins had their Culte de la Raison and Culte de l'Être supreme. The Nazis (National Socialists) had their neo-pagan mysticism. Communists in Russia, China, North Korea, Cuba, and Romania have their personality cults. And, whatever their disagreements among themselves, they've always taken great pains to eradicate rival cults.

All politics is ultimately religion, and, in the course of history, Protestantism fractured Christendom, advanced secularism, and ensured the replacement of Catholic inquisitors with leftist ones—and no Christian can match a secular leftist for persecuting zeal. The Left champions "tolerance" and "free speech" when it is weak, but quickly dumps these positions when it is strong. Tolerance, we should remember, is not a virtue. Tolerance is indifference to the truth—and it is *that* indifference which helps the Left gain power. Conservatives who bemoan leftist intolerance and hypocrisy on free speech are missing the point and being outmaneuvered. Virtually no one wants free speech for bigots. All the Left has to do—and what the Left inevitably does—is define conservatives as bigots. Then "free speech" and "tolerance" for conservatives ends. The issue is not free speech and tolerance, it is right and wrong.

Once the Left gains power, it operates without mercy, because mercy is a Christian virtue, not a liberal one. Mercy is conviction—love of justice and truth—tempered by charity. Mercy disappears as Christianity retreats. It is often replaced by the rule of "reason" removed from experience, and "science"—as if this were sacred writ rather than evolving observation. Together, reason and science are meant to put us on "the right side of history." (That's history as written by the Left, of course). That is why the "woke" are so self-righteous, because they have no charity—because they assume their opponents are ignorant, irrational, unscientific hindrances to progress. It is the same view that justified the French terror and the Soviet labor camps; it is the view that drives Big Tech's censorship of dissenting opinion and the "cancel culture" of the woke.

There is only one way to stop them. We must return to the ideals of Christendom. We must return to charity. We must return to Christianity as our organizing principle, at least as envisioned by America's founding fathers. In short, conservatives need to become reactionaries.

CHAPTER FIVE

Why Reactionaries Don't "Follow the Science"

One can point to the Galileo trial,
after which the Church "lost the cosmos."
—Seyyed Hossein Nasr

I'm what's called a Young Earth Creationist. I believe God made the whole universe over a six-day period. By the seventh, when the Lord took his rest, everything—the plants and the animals, the rocks and the clouds, the moon and the stars, and (most important) man himself—existed in more or less the same form as they do today.

At least, that's what I tell people.

The truth is that I haven't the faintest idea whether the universe was created in seven days or seventy billion years. I've devoted no serious time or thought to the question because it doesn't interest me. From what I know of astronomy and physics—that is, nothing at all—the Young Earth Creationist account seems as plausible as any other. So, when the question arises, that's the answer I give.

What interests me far more is seeing how people react when I say I'm a Young Earth Creationist. Usually, it's with some mixture of horror, anger, and disgust.

Now, I'm not a troll. I never say anything just to rile someone up. I say what I believe to be true; if it does rile someone up, that's just a bonus. But why should it? Whether I believe the earth was made by God or the Big Bang or the Emperor Xenu has no effect on anyone else's life whatsoever. In fact, it has no effect on my life either, which is why I don't bother about it. Yet the conversation always unsettles people.

Mind you, I don't spend much time with cosmologists. The folks I'm talking with have about the same expertise that I do—that is, none whatsoever.[1] I'm sure that, like me, the only thing they remember of studying evolution in school is the Scopes Monkey Trial. That's when the dumb Christians tried and failed to prevent the smart people from teaching real science in schools.

The people who write textbooks that discuss the Scopes Trial generally aren't cosmologists either. But that doesn't matter. Our schools don't teach students about evolution: they inform them of it. To deny evolution or the Big Bang is the equivalent of denying gravity. Evolution is part of our mental furniture. It's just there. It's taken for granted. It's been there for so long, we can't imagine what the place would look like without it. Likewise, for many of us, the Big Bang. We accept all this on faith, and then never think much about it ever again.

It's no revelation that our moribund education system fills children's heads with things they don't care about, can't understand, and will never use at any point in their lives. More interesting is the question of why people not well instructed in science are hostile to other people not well instructed in science, but who have different ideas.

To answer that question, we must consult Dr. John Dewey. In his lifetime, Dewey became a household name as the father of the modern education system. He's also known as the principal theorist of pragmatism, a philosophy that categorically rejects metaphysics; another name for pragmatism is "radical empiricism."

Dewey's adventures in educational "reform" had a dual purpose. One was a genuine desire to improve the lot of ordinary men by making them more intelligent. The other was far more malicious. He aimed to purge all unscientific thoughts from children's brains before they could grow up to become superstitious, fundamentalist bigots— or, in common parlance, Christians.

"Education is a social process," Dewey declared; "education is growth; education is not preparation for life but is life itself." And religion had no place in the life of a progressive, educated man of the twentieth century.

Under the Deweyite regime, schools have become little more than propaganda mills for pragmatism. That's why teachers (especially in public schools) are so hostile to any whiff of the supernatural. It runs contrary to the education establishment's self-proclaimed mission: to create enlightened and efficient citizens of our liberal modernity. Most teachers couldn't care less if their students understand the cosmic microwave background or natural selection. They don't understand them themselves. The point is that children should be incapable of conceiving a universe that is not perfectly explicable by natural phenomena. They might be allowed a theory of God as some idle watchmaker in the sky, as the deists thought of him. But there must always be a voice somewhere in the back of their minds which says, "Whether or not God exists, he certainly isn't necessary."

Unfortunately, my own beloved Catholic Church has been quick to accommodate itself to the Deweyites. Rather than attack the Deweyite secular ideology and its state-sponsored propaganda campaign, most of our apologists are content to solemnly chant the names of Catholic scientists such as Nicolaus Copernicus and Gregor Mendel, hoping to win God a little airtime and show that the Church really isn't hostile to science, but actually helped found science in its universities.

Now, I'm not arguing that the Church should embrace creationism or abandon science. I'm not in the habit of telling my mother what to think, let alone my Holy Mother Church. But it's painful to watch the best Catholic minds of our generation begging for scraps from the pragmatists' table.

It wasn't always this way.

Consider the case of Cardinal Robert Bellarmine: saint, Doctor of the Church, and hero of the Counter-Reformation. Bellarmine is best known today, however, as the judge who presided at the trials of Galileo Galilei. He's universally accepted as the archetype of the superstitious medieval prelate who tried to smother the Scientific Revolution in its crib before it could pose a real threat to the clericalist regime. Nothing could be further from the truth.

As it happens, Galileo himself asked that Bellarmine consider his case. The two had met at least once before, and Galileo clearly trusted the man. Bellarmine's judgment was modest and prudent: by the scientist's own admission, Bellarmine had simply said (and I quote): "Content yourself to speak hypothetically and not absolutely." In other words, Galileo was free to advocate his theories, but only as *theories*, not facts, because his theories weren't yet proven.

Why would Bellarmine make such a judgment? First, because Galileo's heliocentric theories were relatively novel in the scientific world. That was the point. Copernicus had already proposed that the sun was at the center of the universe, but it remained a minority view—held by a small minority at that. Virtually every scientist consulted by Galileo's prosecutors would have affirmed that Galileo was either foolish, arrogant, or malicious.

Second, and more important, medieval Christians assumed that the earth was the center of creation. Bellarmine knew that this belief was becoming a debatable proposition and was clearly prepared for the Church to reconcile herself to heliocentrism, should Galileo prove his theories. But he couldn't allow one man with a telescope to overturn the entire medieval cosmos only to find a hundred years later that he'd made some error in his star charts. The world needed *time*: time to come to terms with the fact that it wasn't the center of the universe. And time is precisely what the scientific method would afford, had Galileo chosen to follow it.

Bellarmine was dealing with a higher truth than mere fact. He wasn't "threatened" by Galileo, as so many historians now claim. On the contrary: he knew that the entire debate was immaterial. The planets would keep turning in the sky with or without mankind's permission. Whether they turned around the earth or the sun or a great wheel of space-cheese called the moon is nothing but a curiosity.

Bellarmine was concerned with a reality far realer than anything Signor Galilei could see through his telescope. What matters most is not earth's position in our galaxy but earth's position with God. Earth is the stage upon which God created his finest artwork: mankind. He gave us ears that we may hear the seas churn as his Spirit broods over the waters. He gave us tongues to taste the fruit trees in their season. He gave us eyes (yes) to wonder at the little fires that burn white-hot in the firmament. When he came down from heaven, he chose to come to earth. When he took on flesh, it was the flesh of earth's steward: man.

In short, Bellarmine was thinking of "The Model": the phrase used by medievalists such as C. S. Lewis to describe the harmony in creation bestowed by its Creator.

"For I will behold thy heavens, the works of thy fingers," King David sings, "the moon and the stars which thou hast founded." This is what Christians believe quite literally, whether they're creationists or evolutionists. We believe that all that exists was made according to God's design. Whatever his methods, God himself beheld his creation and thought it was good.

No one believes in The Model anymore (except for reactionaries like me, of course). But the basic idea of *harmony* within creation has survived to this day, which is why Galileo's true enemies, such as the Dominican friar Niccolò Lorini, were wrong to suppose that his theories would bring down the Catholic Church.[2] It's just that linking the harmony of creation to Christianity has become more elusive now—more mysterious. Once, it was as plain as an apple falling to the ground. Now, it's more like the moon turning the tides.

Looking back at how medieval man thought of the universe—so orderly and well-defined—Lewis remarked: "He is like a man being conducted through an immense cathedral, not like one lost on a shoreless sea." As for us moderns—who hasn't looked up at the night sky and once or twice felt a twinge of horror? The medieval man contemplated the heavens; we "enlightened" men stare into a void.

And here is the crucial point. Bellarmine wasn't afraid that man would lose his faith in God. He was afraid, rather, that man would lose faith in himself.

Christians quickly reconciled to the fact that God had placed the sun at the center of the universe (as they knew it). What they didn't understand was *why*. It seemed as if they were not, to use the horrible modern phrase, special. Clearly, God had done a great deal for them, but earth appeared to be a sideshow. His attention was elsewhere. Once, the night sky had been a veil, shielding man from God's awful glory, but adorned with little rents through which shined Divine Intelligence. Suddenly, it seemed more like an empty church with votive candles flickering in the darkness, the priest away somewhere on more important business. Mankind still needed God, that was clear. It just didn't seem as though he had much need for men.

Western man has long since reconciled himself to his place in the universe. But that first rupture was so jarring, so total, that we've never really managed to shake that sense of cosmic loneliness. It drove atheists such as H. P. Lovecraft mad, while inspiring Christians such as C. S. Lewis to imagine other Christs redeeming other planets. The world, which seemed so absurd to men such as Albert Camus, led Evelyn Waugh to find God in the relationships and experiences of men. Others, such as T. S. Eliot, turned inward: a somewhat bathetic experiment known as high modernism. A few, such as Father Hopkins, still managed to hear those celestial bodies ringing in their orbit. But for most—even those, such as Chesterton, who longed desperately to hear them—they suddenly fell silent. There persists a feeling of humanity's estrangement from nature, even human nature.

Not since the end of the Middle Ages have we met a man such as Saint Francis, who felt at one with all creation, and we may never do so again. We'll likely never see another Chaucer, who moved with such perfect ease through the world. We can appreciate the genius of Dante, but heaven and hell are very different to us than they were to the medieval man. To him, hell inspired real dread and heaven true delight. But to us, lost in the cosmos, the afterlife is something we can't begin to fathom. A hell or heaven outside of time and space doesn't seem like life at all.

For the medieval man, the universe was large enough to inspire awe, but he felt at home within it. We moderns feel lost even in our own bodies.

All of this Robert Bellarmine foresaw. He knew that, given time, man would learn to appreciate his true place in the cosmos. Alas, we never had the chance. After the Scientific Revolution, Protestant polemicists used the temporary suppression of Galileo's ideas as yet another cudgel with which to beat the Catholic Church. That attack did less to advance Protestantism than it did to advance secularism, because as the Scientific Revolution advanced, it didn't raise science up: it tore everything *but* science down.

Charles Darwin seemed to have fun traipsing about the Galapagos Islands looking at turtles and birds, but now even that much is closed to us. Science has become a realm of applied mathematics. As Galileo himself said, "The book of Nature is written in the language of mathematics," and most scientists today are occupied with complicated math problems. Their work has little to do with nature, because nature itself, as per Galileo, has become little more than a math problem. That gravity makes things go down and not sideways, we're told, is the result of a celestial explosion that happened fourteen billion years ago. Everything developed from that first event as a matter of chance, which can be calculated through computer modeling.

We pretend to be excited about science because we're trained to believe in nothing else. The flaw in the Scientific Revolution was not the science, but the revolution. It set out to free us from superstition and only succeeded in plunging us into a hideous skepticism from which we have never emerged. Modern man finds it hard to shake the suspicion that he's merely a brain floating in a vat. That isn't progress. It isn't "humanism." It's *anti*-humanism. Life is no longer a *mysterium tremendum et fascinans* but a cruel and rambling joke.

"Like Saturn," Mallet du Pan observed, "the Revolution devours its children." That's as true of the Scientific Revolution as it was of the French Revolution. The radical skepticism engendered by the Scientific Revolution has now brought science itself into question. In 2020, the Smithsonian Institution claimed that "emphasis on the scientific method," including "objective, rational linear thinking" and "cause and effect relationships," is merely an "assumption of whiteness." In other words, science is a Western construct. It has no objective value; it may even encourage white supremacism. If science is not the pursuit of how God ordered the universe; if science—with all its theories and methods—exists only in our minds, which are themselves reducible to the random firing of synapses in the brain, then, who knows, perhaps through their genetic inheritance Europeans have developed minds more in line with "objective, rational linear thinking" than others. If God-given objective truth is nonsense, a non sequitur, then there is no reason why this genetic development, if it is one, should be "privileged" over others; science, in short, is racism. This way madness lies. Even Richard Dawkins, a scientific evangelist for atheism, has found himself targeted by the "cancel culture" for not sharing the full revolutionary agenda—but then again, how could he share it, when the revolutionary agenda is still working itself out?

The reactionary regards Bellarmine—like Savonarola—as a hero. Bellarmine understood man in his fullness; he did not reduce him to atoms. He understood the greater truths about God and man that the dead, dull, literal way of looking at life that is scientism ignores, crushing out man's own humanity.

CHAPTER SIX

Why Reactionaries Don't Worship Reason

Mine was not an Enlightened mind, I now was aware: it was a Gothic mind, medieval in its temper and structure. I did not love cold harmony and perfect regularity of organization; what I sought was variety, mystery, tradition, the venerable, the awful.

—Russell Kirk

This is a curious fact of our history: Every counter-revolutionary movement—be it the Scottish Jacobites, the French legitimists, or the Spanish Carlists—has equally emphasized two principles: authority and liberty, believing that the two are inextricably bound together. The feudalism of the past protected freedom and independence, because there was no central government. Kings held virtually no power outside of their personal vassals. A king's main duty was to coordinate the defense of the realm and defend the Church within the kingdom. That's why kings rode at the front of their armies: the code of chivalry demanded that the most powerful men also be the bravest and most valiant of men. Chivalry further demanded that the nobility uphold Christian ideas of justice, and the nobility acted as a check on the king. As Chesterton noted, even if a feudal king acted tyrannically, he "hanged and burned in quite a small way." For all their Enlightenment boasts, the democratizing and liberalizing movements of the eighteenth century made our governments prey to tyrants who could hang and burn in quite a larger way.

In the Middle Ages, statecraft was regarded as precisely that: a craft, a trade, like cabinetmaking or glassblowing. Remember, this was before the advent of ideology. Europe's moral, religious, and social views were almost uniform from England to Russia. There was no competition between political sects with competing "philosophies."

Sovereigns learned their trade the same way glassmakers did: by studying at the feet of their fathers. A prince was an apprentice to a king, learning the family trade. He was initiated into the mysteries of statecraft by living and working in his workshop, the palace. He observed his father's dealings with generals and ambassadors, lords spiritual and temporal. In this sense, classical monarchy was also a kind of technocracy, but it was technê of the best kind: not the mundane calculations of a bureaucrat, but the practice of a master artisan.

The purview of the state was also far more limited than it is today. Society was astonishingly well-regulated by what we now call NGOs, or non-governmental organizations. The Church policed moral and social norms. Guilds provided for a fair and well-balanced economy. Religious orders maintained and, in fact, invented universities, hospitals, and other humane ventures. Society was organized around small, self-sufficient institutions (what Burke called "little platoons") that enjoyed vast local autonomy (as with the Carlists' demand for "fueros!"). Best of all, the mass of men, the serfs, were still mostly self-sufficient farmers. They paid their little taxes to their lairds and were otherwise left alone.

So, there was very little for the king to do. He had three jobs, broadly speaking. The first was to safeguard liberties of the Church, the guilds, and the other institutions of the realm. The second was to secure the peace of the realm. The third, and most important, was to serve as the father of his people. He was the *patriarcha*: the patriarch of his family, the nation.

Medieval kings took very seriously this idea of *patriarcha*: the national family united under the sovereign's headship. The subject had a filial duty to serve and honor his king, but the king also had a paternal duty to protect and provide for his subjects. As Saint Thomas Aquinas observes in *De Regno*: "The aim of any ruler should be directed towards securing the welfare of that which he undertakes to rule." Bishop Bossuet—the greatest defender of classical monarchy in history—advised his prince, "Nothing is so royal as to be the help of him who has none.... Among the people, those for whom the prince must provide most are the weak; for they have greater need of him who is, by his charge, the father and protector of all." Juan Donoso Cortés, in his *Essays on Catholicism, Liberalism, and Socialism*, recalls the Church's traditional words to Christian princes upon their ascending the throne:

> Receive this scepter as an emblem of the sacred power confided to you in order that you may protect the weak, sustain the wavering, correct the vicious, and conduct the good in the way of salvation. Receive this scepter as the rule of divine justice, which upholds the good and punishes the wicked; learn by it to love justice, and to abhor iniquity.

That's sound advice for any patriarch, whether he heads a household or a kingdom.

Of course, there's a world of difference between a true patriarchy and the modern nanny state. The nanny state, as the name suggests, babies its citizens. It has erected a massive welfare system like a crib to protect its charges from any inconvenience or discomfort. It provides its children, the people, with a constant supply of oil, which they suck down like mother's milk, and shiny, useless trinkets to keep them entertained. But that crib, in time, acts like a cage; the children don't have room to stretch their legs, to work their muscles. They grow up stunted and weak, utterly dependent on their nurse. When the schoolyard bully takes their bottles and their toys, nanny sends an army to get them back. But if the army is made up of stunted, overgrown infants, it might not do such a good job.[1]

The usual (perhaps the only) argument against a Christian monarchy is, "What if the king is mad?" The answer, of course, is, "He very well might be." But that doesn't mean, as republicans suppose, that the king will wake up one day and decide to massacre his own subjects. That never happened in Christian Europe. Not only did the inclination not exist, but neither did the infrastructure; the king's power was too limited, checked as it was by the nobles and the Church. No, in a Christian monarchy the worst you get is a king such as Ludwig II of Bavaria, who spent such inordinate sums building castles that his ministers tried to remove him from power.

Genocide is the great vice of republics, not monarchies. If a medieval king wanted to slaughter his own people en masse—which, of course, he wouldn't—how would he go about it? There would be no standing army or federal police force to carry out his bidding. If poor King John had decided to massacre a group of Lancastrians, he would have had to petition the Duke of Lancaster; the Duke of Lancaster would then have had to order the knights of Lancaster to slaughter the Lancastrian serfs. Now, if the duke and his troops didn't refuse King John for mercy's sake, they would have refused out of self-interest. Without serfs to work the fields, they would have nothing to eat.

Alternatively, the Duke of Lancaster could assent to John's order, promise to kill his own vassals—and then simply not do it. How would John know, aside from discovering a few years later that the duke hadn't starved to death? There was no domestic intelligence agency, no census bureau, no federal reserve to track the peasant demographic. John would have to ride out personally and survey the entire duchy. If he found it suspiciously well-peopled, the duke could simply say, "Well, you should've come 'round before! This place was practically crawling with peasants. I had my reservations at first, but it really opened things up nicely."

The nearest we come to genocide in the Middle Ages is the Spanish Inquisition, which executed nearly half the number of people every year as the state of Texas does today.[2]

How did we go from these benign feudal kingdoms to the totalitarian regimes of Hitler and Stalin? There were economic factors, of course, but the main political factor was the rise of ideology.

What is ideology? A suitable definition may be "the divorce of *epistêmê* from *technê*"—of ideas from action, of theory from praxis. A fuller definition would be "an inversion of philosophy; an anti-philosophy." Philosophy, in its classic sense, is the love of, and pursuit of, wisdom. It seeks to understand reality so far as we are able, and to humble ourselves so far as we are not. Ideology is just the opposite, and it has largely displaced philosophy among the educated classes. It is an attempt to make all of creation fully intelligible to human reason—to squeeze reality into a narrow set of theories and dogmas.

Ideology is a product of the Enlightenment and began (naturally) as a political force. The *philosophes*, being men of leisure and learning, thought they could devise a system of government that would be fairer and more effective than classical monarchy. That is to say, they felt they could rule France better than the Bourbons and that they could do so on the basis of reason alone, which would guide them in establishing just and equitable laws.

Most of their contemporaries rightly found that notion laughable. Remember, government was still considered a craft—light on the *epistêmê*, heavy on the *technê*, and best learned by a long apprenticeship. It wasn't something you could learn by going to a university. Imagine if a group of men in black robes and mortarboard hats walked into a garage and said, "I've read a lot of books and can safely say I know how to fix cars better than you do. If you'll all step into my lecture hall, I'd like to give you a lesson in Aristotle's *Physics* that will improve your work." That's more or less how the Enlightenment sounded to ordinary Frenchmen.

Yet this example still won't do the trick. We have inherited the post-Enlightenment assumption that men of letters are somehow more intelligent than mechanics. In his essay "The Future of the Intelligentsia," that troublesome reactionary Charles Maurras explained that, before the Enlightenment, writers were thought to have one purpose: "Letters served their function as an adornment of the world. It strove to soften, polish, and amend common manners. They were the interpreters and, as it were, the voices of love, the sting of pleasure, the enchantment of long winters and old age."

The fact is, the talents of writers and academics, though laudable, have nothing to do with statecraft. Why, then, do we place so much weight in the opinions of intellectuals—men whose trade it is to read and write? During the Enlightenment, "reason" was the answer, and a sufficient number of Frenchmen took their politics from these over-educated fops—these "deep coquettes," as Maurras called them—to overthrow the Kingdom of France.

As the seventeenth and eighteenth centuries progressed, the idea that intellectuals formed a kind of universally competent elite began to take hold. Even those who decried the new intelligentsia, such as Edmund Burke and Joseph de Maistre, had to adopt their methods. So, even the opponents of ideology became ideologists themselves. Peter Viereck defined conservatism as the "revolt against ideology," but that revolt, like every other ideology, needed an -ism of its own. Slovenian philosopher Slavoj Žižek is wrong to say that everything is ideology, but it's true that, in the modern world, everyone is an ideologue.

Except, of course, the reactionary. Only he can transcend the confines of ideology by (as C. S. Lewis says) "going back till he finds the error and working it afresh from that point." Only by grounding himself firmly in the past can he raise himself over three centuries' worth of putrid theorizing. Most of what we call philosophy today is nothing but word games played by men with too much confidence in their own rational powers. It is, as Maistre says, "an essentially destructive force." It confounds understanding rather than increasing it. It dismisses wisdom as superstition and destroys understanding by skepticism. Today, the only true philosopher is the reactionary.

Coincidentally, the original ideologists—the *philosophes* of the Enlightenment—were republicans and democrats. They agreed that man, given his rational powers, is capable of self-government in some shape or form. As ideology spread throughout Christendom, these rationalist and individualist assumptions replaced the old feudal faith in Throne and Altar.

I say "coincidentally" because it is by no means given that a society, upon emerging from feudalism, will become liberal. This is the "end of history" thesis posited by Francis Fukuyama, who himself is the final incarnation of the Whig version of history, which holds not only that societies inevitably evolve in a liberal way (which is progress), but that all societies want to be liberal. History and current experience would tell us that this is manifestly not the case; there's no reason why our first ideologues should have been liberals. In

Russia, for instance, the feudal order was immediately succeeded by communism. Lenin and Stalin were far more autocratic than any tsar, and their somewhat tsarist successor, Vladimir Putin, is far more popular in Russia than many elected leaders are in the liberal West.

In any event, our "ideologization" did happen to be liberal, democratic, and republican. It took individual liberty and self-government as its cornerstone. But by giving the government—the state—a "popular mandate," we allowed and even encouraged it to grow beyond anything dreamt of in Hobbes's philosophy. We sincerely believed that the government was of the people, by the people, and for the people. We granted it privileges beyond anything entailed by the divine right of kings. So long as a liberal government can plausibly claim to be acting within a "popular mandate," its powers are unlimited; it can continually find more things to do, more powers to take on. Indeed, during the COVID-19 pandemic, it was widely assumed that the power of liberal, democratic governments was near absolute. Where it was restrained—as in the United States by federalism—liberal commentators lamented our inability to enforce communist Chinese levels of coercion.

Should this have surprised us? Not really. It surprised the reactionary not at all. Government feels justified in doing all this because it does so in our name. The reactionary thinks we should take our name—and our freedom and independence—back.

CHAPTER SEVEN

Why a Reactionary Would Like to Abolish Politics

My principles are only those that, before the French Revo-
lution, every well-born person considered
sane and normal.
—Julius Evola

S avonarola welcomed the French invasion of Florence in 1494,
addressing King Charles VIII as "God's scourge" sent to cleanse
the city of its voluptuousness. Joseph de Maistre felt the same
way about the Jacobins.

And little wonder. The French Revolution occurred because the
bonds of feudal loyalty had been severed. The French aristocracy
had transgressed its duty to the serfs and, like the Tudors in England, used Romanized laws from the Renaissance to abuse them.
For the better part of three hundred years, the French elite did little
except dress in powdered wigs and high heels, prance about in
gauche palaces, fill their dainty gardens with Hellenic idols, and
centralize power in the Bourbon kings, around whom was built a
cult of personality that included the infamous levee ceremonies,
where lords of the realm competed for the privilege of emptying
the king's chamber pot in the morning.[1]

Maistre hated the Jacobins' politics and their blasphemous republic but was convinced they were only a temporary inconvenience. Once France had repented of its sins, Divine Providence would restore the monarchy and give the House of Bourbon a second chance to rule justly and moderately.

In the meantime, the Jacobins came as a judgment on an elite that had used its power and privilege to exploit the people. And so, reflecting on the Reign of Terror, Maistre declared coldly, "It has been a long time since we have seen such frightful punishment inflicted on such a large number of guilty people. No doubt there are innocents among the unfortunate victims, but they are far fewer than commonly imagined."

I suspect he had in mind men such as Louis Philippe II, Duke of Orléans. When the Revolution broke out, the duke changed his name to "Philippe Égalité" and declared himself for the Jacobins. He voted for the execution of his cousin, Louis XVI—and then was guillotined himself a few months later.

Philippe was typical of the Ancien Régime in that his ambition and selfishness bordered on the sadistic. Maybe he had read Machiavelli's *Discourses on Livy* and believed that, during a revolution, the elite class can best maintain its power by throwing in its lot with the revolutionaries. He pined for a constitutional monarchy like Britain's—which he, of course, would rule as a monarch. Meanwhile, British conservatives such as Edmund Burke completely misunderstood the corrupt House of Bourbon as representing "the age of chivalry." What the Ancien Régime really represented was the repudiation of chivalry. The cruelty and depravity of the French aristocracy were such that one could not really mourn the death of its members.

Still, most French reactionaries didn't share Maistre's faith that Providence would restrain the Jacobins. They (rightly) assumed that the Jacobins would not only punish the debased French ruling class;

their policies of rape and rapine would lay waste the country, pillage the Church, and destroy France's traditional way of life.

Even so, some later reactionaries, such as G. K. Chesterton and Hilaire Belloc, picked up and expanded on Maistre's early support for the Revolution, praising the revolutionaries' commitment to the equality of men. This, as Belloc points out, is a dogma of the Christian faith, and it had been forgotten by those French aristocrats who treated France as their own private brothel.

Even so, Belloc remained a monarchist. Indeed, Belloc saw monarchical power in Britain as a necessary corrective to a political system increasingly dominated by monied interests. Two years after resigning from Parliament in despair, Belloc penned an essay in the *Oxford and Cambridge Review* arguing that the

> increase in the personal power of the monarch is the one real alternative present before the English state today to the conduct of affairs by organized wealth. To the end of increasing the personal power of the king should be directed the efforts of those who fear most what may be called, in one aspect, plutocracy, in another aspect, servitude.

He's right, of course. And this is the exact same argument made by French royalists, who warned that, however corrupt the Ancien Régime might have been, the rule of middle-class radicals would be infinitely worse. (Apparently Belloc never put two and two together, because he never walked back his unconditional support for the French Revolution. C'est la vie.)

In his book *Leftism Revisited*, Erik von Kuehnelt-Leddihn wrote, "For the average person, all problems date to World War II; for the more informed, to World War I; for the genuine historian, to the French Revolution." For the reactionary, it goes back much further than that, because he knows that the Jacobins did not just fall from the sky. He knows the French Revolution was the culmination of several other "turnings" in the Western world, including most especially the re-paganization (and corruption of morals) of the elite that began in the Renaissance, the ruling class's subsequent scorn and abuse of the common man, and the rise of the Cult of Reason.

The French Revolution was the advent of government-by-ideology. It was the logical end of the Enlightenment. Its logical executor was inevitably not a *philosophe* but a genius administrator and dictator named Napoleon.

In his essay *Bourbons and Buonapartes*, François-René de Chateaubriand rightly casts Napoleon as the founding father of the administrative state. "In ten years he devoured fifteen billion in taxes," Chateaubriand notes, "which surpasses the sum levied during the seventy-three years of the reign of Louis XIV." What's more:

> We have praised Buonaparte's administration. If administration consists in numerals, if, to govern well, it suffices to know how much a province produces in wheat, wine, and oil, what is the last penny one may levy as tax, the last man one may take, then certainly Buonaparte was a great administrator. It is impossible better to organize evil or put more order into disorder. But if the best administration is that which leaves the people in peace, which nourishes their sentiments of justice and piety, which is frugal with the blood of men, which respects the rights of citizens, their properties and their families, then certainly the government of Buonaparte was the worst of governments.

Another royalist, Pierre Paul Royer-Collard, made the same point even more powerfully. "We have seen the old society perish," he lamented, "and with it that crowd of domestic institutions and independent magistracies which it carried within it."

These institutions he called "true republics within the monarchy." And these little republics

> did not, it is true, share sovereignty; but they opposed to it everywhere limits which were defended obstinately. Not one of them has survived. The revolution has left only individuals standing. It has dissolved even the (so to speak) physical association of the commune. This is a spectacle without precedent! Before now one had seen only in philosophers' books a nation so decomposed and reduced to its ultimate constituents.
>
> From an atomized society has emerged centralization. There is no need to look elsewhere for its origin. Centralization has not arrived with its head erect, with the authority of a principle; rather; it has developed modestly, as a consequence, a necessity. Indeed, where there are only individuals, all business which is not theirs is necessarily public business, the business of the state. Where there are no independent magistrates, there are only agents of central power. That is how we have become an administered people, under the hand of irresponsible civil servants, themselves centralized in the power of which they are agents.

Let's consider very carefully what's being argued here. In the immediate aftermath of the Revolution, these two reactionaries were already complaining that the state had grown more powerful. The bureaucracy had expanded. All consequential decisions were being made from Paris. More than ever before, the central administration directed every aspect of French public life.

Of course, the new administrators governed according to "Enlightened" theories of applied reason. Educated opinion was on the side of the Nouveau Régime, while the common Frenchman suffered a loss of freedom and independence. That's not a romantic myth, it's the eyewitness testimony of men who watched their government grow to an unprecedented scale. And this expansion of state power wouldn't have been possible without the Revolution.

How did the revolutionaries achieve this power grab? How did they manage to usurp more authority than the Sun King? The answer is quite simple: the government claimed to act in the people's name.

Medieval kings believed they were appointed by God; they believed in divine right, but also in sacred duty, which made them accountable to God. They were vested with authority, but part of that authority was to uphold justice and defend the sacred liberties of their people.

Not so with the Nouveau Régime. Because the governing authorities in a liberal state are (ostensibly) chosen by the people, the rulers are given full license to command the people as they see fit. Their power doesn't exist in any sort of ancestral trust, as in the Middle Ages. There's no sense of duty among modern rulers as there was under feudalism. And there are far fewer intermediary institutions between the individual and the state, except where federalism still exits as a modest restraining power. Instead, we now have a "social contract." Whatever liberties the government usurps, its functionaries will remind us: you signed on the dotted line.

The ratification of this "social contract" has led to an explosion of state power in the last two hundred years. But the power of bureaucrats to direct public life was only the beginning. It also erased any distinction between the public and the private.

The social critic George Steiner (no counterrevolutionary, he!) observed that the Revolution "abolished the millennial barrier between common life and the enormities of the historical. Past the hedge and gate of even the humblest garden march the bayonets of political ideology and historic conflict."

Suddenly, everyone had to have an opinion on politics, whether he liked it or not. In a monarchy, only one man is forced to bear the burdens of state, and, as the Bard says, "uneasy lies the head that wears a crown." In a republic, the crown is divided into a hundred million pieces. We each pin a little shard to our hats, and none of us lie easily; in our politicized age, ideology infects everything. Everything.

This, I think, is the best argument for monarchy. It is not the divine right of kings to rule arbitrarily, but the divine right of men to be ruled competently and modestly.

The question then is not: How do we go about restoring monarchy in this country? That misses the point. The whole point of reactionary politics is to minimize the political. We aim to put the state in its place, which is as far away from the commoner as possible.

"So," you say, "the reactionary is a libertarian?" That's an easy mistake to make, and it's been made by greater minds than my own: Kuehnelt-Leddihn and Joseph Sobran, to name two. But libertarianism is still an ideology. Where the socialist worships the state as a god, the libertarian fears it like a devil. Burke was right on this point, at least: government is "a contrivance of human wisdom to provide for human wants"—nothing more and nothing less.

The libertarian makes the same error regarding the state that pacifists make towards the military or secularists towards the clergy. The libertarian thinks that because government has done bad things in the past, government is fundamentally and irredeemably evil. That is ideological thinking: reducing broad and complicated histories into little bite-sized dogmas.

What Russell Kirk said of conservatives is also true of reactionaries: "Conservatives have no intention of compromising with socialists;

but even such an alliance, ridiculous though it would be, is more nearly conceivable than the coalition of conservatives and libertarians. The socialists at least declare the existence of some sort of moral order; the libertarians are quite bottomless."

The reactionary's love of freedom and authority is not easily labeled. Max Beerbohm came close when he called himself a Tory anarchist: "I should like every one to go about doing just as he pleased, short of altering any of the things to which I have grown accustomed." George Orwell used the phrase to describe Jonathan Swift as one "despising authority while disbelieving in liberty, and preserving the aristocratic outlook while seeing clearly that the existing aristocracy is degenerate and contemptible."

Better was J. R. R. Tolkien's description of himself as an "anarcho-monarchist," because anarcho-monarchism is a philosophy not for aristocrats but for the peasants, the reactionary's natural allies and constituency. The anarcho-monarchist does not despise authority: he longs for it. What he despises is the tyranny exercised by virtually all regimes not founded on divine right. Men who feel they've somehow earned power are far more likely to exercise it badly than a man who credits his throne to God, with sacred responsibilities, and who knows that what the Lord giveth, he may also taketh away.

So it was that Tolkien wrote in a letter to his son Christopher:

> My political opinions lean more and more to Anarchy (philosophically understood, meaning the abolition of control not whiskered men with bombs)—or to 'unconstitutional' Monarchy....
>
> The proper study of Man is anything but Man; and the most improper job of any man, even saints (who at any rate were at least unwilling to take it on), is bossing other men. Not one in a million is fit for it, and least of all those

who seek the opportunity. At least it is done only to a small group of men who know who their master is. The mediaevals were only too right in taking nolo episcopari as the best reason a man could give to others for making him a bishop. Grant me a king whose chief interest in life is stamps, railways, or race-horses; and who has the power to sack his Vizier (or whatever you dare call him) if he does not like the cut of his trousers.

A very sensible view, that. But I think we might also benefit from a more esoteric reading.

The two parts of Tolkien's politics—anarchism and monarchism—represent those two hemispheres of the reactionary brain: the one that loves liberty and the one that longs for authority. One harbors the desire to be left alone; the other, a grim suspicion that we must leave our hobbit-holes and put the world right. It is a hatred of meddling, but also an understanding that we must actively un-meddle, undo the damage done by the chronically meddlesome. The modern reactionary task is the same chivalric task it has always been: to live loyally and joyfully and, when necessary, to fight the profane meddlers.

CHAPTER EIGHT

Reactionary Working Man; Paging Ned Ludd

*The evil that machinery is doing is not merely in the con-
sequence of its work but in the fact that it makes men
themselves machines also.*
—Oscar Wilde

T oo much refinement can be a dangerous thing. No less than our friend Maistre warned against "the gangrenous vices that follow an excess of civilization." Still, when taken in moderate doses, civilization can be a good thing. To that end, we may distinguish between a tool and a machine. A tool is something that allows men to exercise their proficiency more effectively, while a machine is something that renders their proficiency redundant. One is civilized; the other, a little *too* civilized.

For instance, a fulcrum is a tool. So is a scaffold. Being able to lift heavy things more easily doesn't stunt a carpenter's creativity. On the contrary. Without the power to lift massive stones hundreds of feet off the ground and stack them one on top of the other, no architect could have dreamed of building Chartres Cathedral. Mankind has a genius for invention. This is part of his nature, not a deviation from it.

Machines are quite another matter. They, too, are products of man's inventive genius. But they don't encourage his creativity; they stifle it.

The classic example must be the stocking frame. A kind of primitive knitting machine, it was central to the Industrial Revolution in England. It was also hated by professional weavers, for two reasons. First, it allowed a weaver to work more quickly. That meant a mill owner didn't need to employ as many workers—which, in turn, meant that many weavers were laid off. Workers competed for an ever-dwindling number of jobs, which drove down wages.

But second, and perhaps more important, it made their work monotonous. It took the skill and artistry out of the trade.

This is what we mean when we say that a machine renders a man's proficiency redundant. He ceases to be a worker altogether and becomes a mere operator. The machine actually does the job. He just pushes the pedals.

In the late 1700s, a weaver named Ned Ludd broke two of these wretched stocking frames in a fit of righteous indignation. This set off a little revolution across England. Dozens, perhaps hundreds, of weavers followed his lead and smashed the machines. It was the first great uprising against automation. It was a revolt against a new system of management that saw workers as replaceable (and, ultimately, disposable) parts in a new mechanized system of production.

The Industrial Revolution meant that work was no longer seen as a creative outlet—a means for men to exercise their creative genius. For the employee, it was just a way to earn a living. For the employer, it was a means to greater profit, and the road to profit was paved by lower wages and machines' replacing workers. Workers themselves became little more than fleshy machines, more delicate and less efficient than their metal counterparts. And such has been the case ever since.

We can hardly overstate the significance of this shift in Western society. Before the Industrial Revolution, all weavers needed was wool, their hands, and a fair bit of know-how. They had tools—needles and whatnot—but these tools were extensions of their hands, not replacements for them. Now workers were replaceable.

Mr. Ludd couldn't set up his own business; he couldn't afford to buy a stocking frame of his own. Only the burgeoning merchant middle class could afford these new machines. And so, the working man was forced to abandon his trade, forget his skills, and settle for a life of pushing pedals for a pittance.

As the mill owners continued their campaign of automation, their wealth grew steadily while the commoners' wages fell and unemployment expanded. Independent weavers couldn't compete with the mills, which meant that owners opened even more mills, turning even more weavers into fleshy machines.

Unsurprisingly, the average worker's quality of life declined along with his quality of work. The skilled independent craftsman was on track to extinction—and, along with him, the skilled and independent freeman.

In time, old Ned lent his name to a movement called Luddism. Today, the word "Luddite" is still used to refer to technophobes, such as yours truly.

Another prominent Luddite was the poet George Gordon, Lord Byron. In 1812, the 6th Baron Byron used his maiden speech to the British House of Lords to oppose Prime Minister Spencer Perceval, who was seeking to make "machine-breaking" a capital offense. Byron was incensed. He insisted that "nothing but absolute want could have driven a large, and once honest and industrious, body of the people, into the commission of excesses so hazardous to themselves, their families, and the community."

"You may call the people a mob," he warned, "but do not forget that a mob too often speaks the sentiments of the people."

Likewise, in his 1816 poem "Song for the Luddites," Byron sang:

As the Liberty lads o'er the sea
Bought their freedom, and cheaply, with blood,
So we, boys, we
Will die fighting, or live free,
And down with all kings but King Ludd!

Byron failed, however, and Perceval succeeded. Less than a month after Byron's maiden speech, a twelve-year-old Luddite named Abraham Charlson was hanged for helping to burn a mill in Lancaster. He cried for his mother as he was led to the gallows.

Industrialism continued apace for over a century. Then, early in the twentieth century, we see the appearance of the Anti-Ludd: Henry Ford.

In his landmark essay for the *New Atlantis*, "Shop Class as Soulcraft," Matthew Crawford recalls how Henry Ford's employees quit en masse when he rolled out his famed assembly line in 1913. Mr. Crawford quotes a Ford biographer: "So great was labor's distaste for the new machine system that toward the close of 1913 every time the company wanted to add 100 men to its factory personnel, it was necessary to hire 963."

Even as late as the early 1900s, men could reasonably expect that their jobs would provide some deeper satisfaction than a mere paycheck. It was an unquestioned rule of American life. To suggest that a grown man should spend his life fitting tires to disc rotors over and over and over again was unthinkable.

Mr. Crawford goes on:

Ford was forced to double the daily wage of his workers to keep the line staffed. As [Harry] Braverman writes, this "opened up new possibilities for the intensification of labor within the plants, where workers were now anxious to keep their jobs." These anxious workers were more productive. Indeed, Ford himself later recognized his wage increase as "one of the finest cost-cutting moves we ever made," as he was able to double, and then triple, the rate at which cars were assembled by simply speeding up the conveyors. By doing so he destroyed his competitors, and thereby destroyed the possibility of an alternative way of working.

Marxists, of course, have their own language for this phenomenon. They say that the bourgeoisie (the middle class) monopolized the means of production (the machines), which led to the proletarianization of the worker (the transformation of skilled artisans into unskilled laborers)—which, in turn, led to the workers' alienation (they got pissed off and started breaking things).

The reactionary is not a Marxist, however, because Marxism doesn't object to proletarianization per se. In fact, the Marxist welcomes it. No less than the capitalist, he embraces the Industrial Revolution as a necessary, if painful, step in mankind's "progress." His complaint isn't that industrialism reduced our view of mankind into *homo economicus*. As an atheist, that's what a Marxist (and many a libertarian) thinks a man is. He'd say that any other view is superstitious or sentimental.

The reactionary, on the contrary, thinks that man is made in the image of God. The goal of the reactionary is the resurrection of skilled craftsmen, the abolition of assembly lines and automation, the restoration of tools and an apprentice system that teaches how to use them. We are Luddites through and through. We believe that workers should own the "means of production"—not collectively, as the Marxists do, but individually, as freemen. We believe in the dignity, liberty, and independence of men earning their living through their own skills.

Is this far-fetched? Maybe. Yet it was just over one hundred years from Byron's maiden speech to Ford's assembly line and the Bolsheviks' bringing Marxism to Russia. Within another hundred years, the Soviet Union had fallen, and those assembly lines had disappeared from America—outsourced to China and Vietnam, where wage slaves living under post-communist regimes worked for pennies on the dollar.

We take all this "progress" for granted. Yet the economic system of family farmers and independent craftsmen born in the Middle Ages lasted for well over a thousand years, while the history of industrialism has undergone countless revolutions and mutations in just two centuries. Whatever else you want to say about it—no matter what you find to praise or blame—our status quo is far from inevitable. Capitalism, no less than communism, is horribly unstable, and no necessary champion of freedom. The reactionary can point to a better way, a tried and tested way, a way that provides happiness and meaningful labor in a world that needs plenty of both.

CHAPTER NINE

The Reactionary American

Here is your country. Cherish these natural wonders, cherish the natural resources, cherish the history and romance as a sacred heritage, for your children and your children's children. Do not let selfish men or greedy interests skin your country of its beauty, its riches or its romance.
—Theodore Roosevelt

I f you've made it this far in the book, you might expect a stinging rebuke of the founding fathers, a rousing defense of absolute monarchy, and maybe a call for some kind of Catholic integralism.

Actually, so did I.

Then I started plunging into medieval history, and two facts kept leaping out at me. First, the greatest kings of Europe weren't absolutists. And, second, the great kingdoms of Europe weren't integralist.

The Middle Ages were a huge, glorious cacophony of competing interest groups. Church and state were constantly vying for dominance. Throne and Altar were seldom at peace. Kings, nobles, and bishops were all jockeying for power over the local fiefdoms. Emperors dueled with popes for influence over the whole Continent.

It's pretty funny, when you think about it. These weren't the powerful nation-states we think of today. Borders were constantly expanding and collapsing. Powerful dukes would overthrow the royal house and install their own kinfolk on the throne. The Church would place whole countries under the interdict, excommunicating the entire population until the sovereign bowed to its will. Kings appointed bishops; bishops voted for popes; popes crowned kings. Compared to (say) World War II, the little feuds of the Feudal Age look like schoolboys getting into a slap-fight on the playground.

But thanks to this constant state of near-anarchy, the locus of power wasn't those great castles or cathedrals. Real authority was found in the avenues of common life: minor liege-lords and humble parish priests, guilds and fraternities, and even a few elected mayors. All government was local government, and all businesses were small businesses.

Which makes perfect sense, when you think about it. When you have such small communities and simple economies, what is there to actually rule? It wasn't until the Age of Exploration and the Industrial Revolution, when international trade and large-scale manufacturing began to boom, that there was a real incentive for rulers to grab more power. The medieval tyrant couldn't horde wealth because there wasn't much wealth to horde.

Europe's economic expansion from the fifteenth century onward precipitated the rise of the bureaucratic state, creating a gulf between the well-off, well-educated elite (including the New Men) and the common man. Europe's culture became less Christian, more commercial, and more worldly.

Out of the many Protestant denominations that emerged from the Reformation, one emerged that was not opposed to commerce, but was very much opposed to the Church of England's remaining Romish tendencies, which it linked to the decadence of the

Renaissance. This was the Puritans, who wanted to purify the Church of England and return the country to godly rule.

I know, I know, it seems odd for a Catholic Jacobite to praise the Puritans, but, in many ways, they were honorable opponents, and today, as Christian denominations come together against aggressive secularism, we can even see them as long-term allies.

The very name Puritan has become a byword for prudery, intolerance, and a spirit of all-around killjoy-ism. Which, to an extent, is fair enough. They did ban Christmas, after all. But they were an interesting, and in many ways admirable, lot.

We could say more about the Puritans' theology, but I think far too much has been said about that already—especially by folks who have no sympathy with their faith whatsoever. Besides, it's not Puritanism as a religious movement that interests me so much as the character of the Puritan men and women who came to America. The Pilgrims, the Puritan separatists from the Church of England who landed at Plymouth in 1620, and the Puritans, who founded the Massachusetts Bay Colony ten years later, were the first and most intrepid of America's pioneers.

The Puritans emigrated to the New World for more than strictly religious reasons; they had broad moral reasons as well. As separatists (and, in the Pilgrims' case, emigrants), they were less concerned with purifying the Church of England than with purifying themselves and founding a purer society. A common theme in Puritan writing is that, despite Christendom's great material success, the West had suffered some grave moral loss. The body was flourishing, but the soul was dying. And, more than any preference for Calvin's neo-Augustinian theory of predestination, it was this sense of loss that spurred the Puritans in their voyage to America.

But don't take my word for it. When the *Arbella* set out for the New World, its leader, the Puritan minister John Winthrop, gave a homily called "A Model of Christian Charity." Many politicians quote Winthrop's line about America being a "city upon a hill," but not many seem to have asked *what* would make this country an example for the rest of the world to follow. For the Reverend Mr. Winthrop, the answer was—well, charity. And so he wrote:

> That which the most in their churches maintain as truth in profession only, we must bring into familiar and constant practice; as in this duty of love, we must love brotherly without dissimulation, we must love one another with a pure heart fervently. We must bear one another's burdens. We must not look only on our own things, but also on the things of our brethren.

The Puritans were appalled that Europe's Christians held charity—the rule of love—"as truth in profession only." It didn't guide their lives. Across the Christian West, the Golden Rule, the Puritans thought, was a dead letter.

Whatever their faults, the Puritans who founded Massachusetts Bay strove to live by the law of love. They sought to build a society that was animated by the commands of Jesus Christ: to love God with their hearts and souls and minds and strength, and to love their neighbors as themselves.

Granted, burning old women at the stake was a funny way of showing that they loved them. But I am not a Puritan. I can still admire the noble ideals with which they founded this country. Europe was *converted* to Christianity, but here in America, Christian charity is the foundation of our public life. It's our first principle.

What the American colonists did was transplant Christendom from the exhausted soil of the Old World into the fresh earth of the New World. Life on that lonely American outpost of civilization—nestled between a cold, churning ocean and an endless, hostile frontier—put a certain manly vigor back in Western culture.

How could it not? Suddenly, these European emigrants found themselves huddled together in small communities, living off the fruits of land and sea. Once again, the squabbles of kings and bishops faded into the background. They were ruled by local ministers and magistrates. They took up arms not to conquer other peoples, but to provide for the common defense. The first Americans were like serfs without lords. They were freemen and peasants all at once.

By necessity, the rule of love was combined with the law of self-reliance. Christ taught us to love our neighbor, yes. But Saint Paul, in his Second Letter to the Thessalonians, added: "Anyone unwilling to work should not eat." And so, in 1609, in an earlier settlement at Jamestown, John Smith warned the English colonists that "the greater part must be more industrious, or starve." Quoting that line from Saint Paul, he declared:

> You must obey this now for a law, that he that will not work shall not eat (except by sickness he be disabled). For the labors of thirty or forty honest and industrious men shall not be consumed to maintain a hundred and fifty idle loiterers.

Clearly, Winthrop and Smith were no soft, luxurious aristocrats. While the colonists didn't follow the rule of chivalry per se, their ministers and magistrates were expected to be model citizens. Colonial rulers had to practice what they preached, and then some.

This "rugged individualism" became the bedrock of what we now know as American culture. And even if New England's settlers had been High-Church Anglicans, their very presence in this untamed land would've forced them to become leaner, tougher, and simpler.

In 1666, the Puritan poetess Anne Bradstreet wrote what I think is the first truly American poem. She gave it the (very economical) title "Verse upon the Burning of Our House." Here's how it ends:

> A price so vast as is unknown,
> Yet by His gift is made thine own;
> There's wealth enough, I need no more,
> Farewell, my pelf, farewell, my store.
> The world no longer let me love,
> My hope and treasure lies above.

Bradstreet was a bigger man than all the dandy poets in all the decadent courts of Europe.

Everything about early America was brutal, right down to the naming of our towns. Take the naming of Barre, Vermont, as recalled by George R. Stewart in his classic study *Names on the Land*. Originally called Wildersburg, the townsfolk eventually got sick of the name and in 1793 called a meeting to choose a new one:

> Captain Joseph Thompson strenuously contended for Holden, in honor of the town in Massachusetts which had been his former home. Mr. Jonathan Sherman was equally vehement for Barre, because he had come from Barre, also in Massachusetts. The argument was so hot that someone proposed a settlement by combat. The champions readily agreed. The meeting then adjourned to a new barn-shed with a floor of rough hemlock planks. Space was cleared, and a pole was leveled waist-high. The combatants were to fight with their fists across this pole; but if one should knock the other down, he might follow up his advantage in any way he could.

Thompson had the upper hand for a while and managed to get Sherman on his back. But Sherman dodged the blows so deftly that the captain only ended up punching the hemlock floor. That spelled doom for Thompson—and the Holdenites. "Sherman, throwing him off, sprang to his feet and claimed the victory by shouting in exultation, 'There, the name is Barre, by God!'"

This medieval spirit survived well into the Founding Era. Most of us think of John Adams as the first American conservative, and he's great. In fact, he was widely denounced by many other founding fathers for arguing that our chief executive (the president) should serve a role like that of the medieval king: a tribune of the masses, defending ordinary Americans against the rich and powerful.

But Thomas Jefferson got the American *thing* best when he said the fundamental unit of our republic is the yeoman farmer, the free peasant. At our best, Americans have always been self-governing serfs.

No doubt the best-known defenders of the Jeffersonian ideal in our age were the Southern Agrarians. Their 1930 manifesto *I'll Take My Stand* remains the best defense of the Old South's commitment to states' rights and its land-based economy published since the Civil War. Southern Agrarian John Crowe Ransom gave a perfect summary of the reactionary's creed when he wrote:

> The concept of Progress is the concept of man's increasing command, and eventually perfect command, over the forces of nature; a concept which enhances too readily our conceit, intoxicates us, and brutalizes our life. I believe it is demonstrable that there is possible no deep sense of beauty, no heroism of conduct, and no sublimity of religion, which is not informed by the humble sense of man's precarious position in the universe.

I can't think of a better summary of what Cardinal Bellarmine was trying to defend against the sneering Galileo: a "humble sense of man's precarious position in the universe." That's a sense one only finds among simple men who live close to the earth. It's the first thing we lose among the comforts of Big Business and the security of Big Government. But it's the beginning of wonder, awe, and gratitude.

That's why our religion quickly became so medieval, in the best sense of the word—and also, I suppose, the worst. The American mind couldn't possibly entertain that illusion about the strict divide between the natural and the supernatural. At our lowest moments, this deep piety manifested itself in superstition and witch hunts. But, at its best, it bred a kind of rustic mysticism not seen since the days of Saint Francis of Assisi.

Take the example of Sarah Bishop, "the Hermitess of Ridgefield." Miss Bishop, who died in 1809, lived most of her life alone in a cave on West Mountain in Connecticut. According to memoirist Samuel G. Goodrich, who knew her when he was a boy, "This strange woman was no amateur recluse. The rock, bare and desolate, was actually her home." On the rare occasion that she wandered into Ridgefield Village, "she never begged, but received such articles as were given to her."

Bishop "was of a highly religious turn of mind," Goodrich writes, "and at long intervals came to our church, and partook of the sacrament." Sometimes she would visit the Goodrich family home, but she refused to eat or speak with her hosts. Yet "she listened intently to the reading of the Bible, and joined with apparent devotion in the morning and evening prayer." Bishop even had a distinctly Franciscan gift for charming animals. "It was said, indeed, that she had domesticated a particular rattlesnake, and that he paid her daily visits. She was accustomed—so said the legend—to bring him milk from the villages, which he devoured with great relish."

If the Yankees were ever to produce a mystic like Saint Francis, she would have to be as proud and shy as our Miss Bishop.

And that brings me to my next point. I'm all for the Southern Agrarians, and I heartily support their war against the false god of Progress. My only quibble with the Southern Agrarians is that they're not especially Southern.

Right up until the Civil War, the dynamic in American society wasn't a progressive North versus the conservative South. Quite the opposite, actually. Before the mid-1800s, the North was dominated by family farms and small-scale fisheries. It was only down south that chattel slavery allowed the planter class to do agriculture on a much larger scale.

Like the ancient Greeks, Southerners viewed slavery as a civilizing force. It was the engine of economic and cultural progress. It afforded them the wealth and leisure needed to pursue the finer things in life. Jefferson himself is a perfect example. Nowhere in the North would you have found a man with enough time or dough to build a neoclassical palace such as Monticello, stock it with ten thousand books, and spend his time editing all the miracles out of the Gospels.

Even after the Revolution, the Southern gentry was self-consciously progressive. It's why Southern aristocrats (such as Jefferson) were so partial to the Jacobins, while stolid, middle-class Yankees (such as Adams) shared Burke's horror at the Reign of Terror. Those Southerners saw us Northerners as puritanical rubes, all huddled together in our little saltboxes, helplessly clinging to Mother England. Which, in fairness, we were.

We all know the North tended towards abolitionism long before the Civil War. But abolitionism wasn't only about treating black folks with more dignity. There was another crucial dynamic at play, as James L. Huston explains in his fascinating book *The British Gentry, the Southern Planter, and the Northern Family Farmer: Agriculture and Sectional Antagonism in North America.*

By and large, Northerners detested chattel slavery for the same reason their Pilgrim ancestors chafed in Renaissance England. They believed the South's plantations bred a cruel, unmanly softness—one wholly at odds with America's tradition of rugged individualism, and which had no place in our "model of charity." Or, as Professor Huston puts it, "The core ideological difference between North and South was neither the free labor ideology nor the patriarchy of the plantation. The clash was between the self-mastery of the family farm and the mastery-over-others of the plantation."

Anyway, it was only when the Industrial Revolution began to take root in Mid-Atlantic states such as Delaware and Rhode Island that the South began to see slavery as a conservative institution—as a pillar of its local traditions, not the engine of progress. And that's where history gets a little tricky.

As much as the Southern planter and the Yankee family-farmer were at odds, they found a common enemy in the developed Northern cities. Commercial ports, such as Boston, and industrial centers, such as Hartford, engendered all of those vices an old-school Yankee despises. They cheapened work, divided the poor and rich, tore up small communities, and encouraged large, centralized governments. Little wonder that rural counties in Massachusetts, New York, Vermont, and New Hampshire produced some of the leading Anti-Federalists. In the decades leading up to 1861, they frequently swung to Jefferson's Democratic-Republican Party.

When the Civil War broke out, the Pilgrims' heirs had to choose sides, and none of them were too pleased about it. Franklin Pierce, the only president to hail from the great state of New Hampshire, reluctantly threw his lot in with the Confederacy; his best friend, the novelist Nathaniel Hawthorne, reluctantly threw his lot in with the

Union. Yet both felt strongly that whichever side "won," America would lose. If the South managed to break away, slavery would limp on indefinitely. But if the North held the Union together, it would crush the South, and the Yankee farmer would have no ally against the rising tide of industrialism and centralism—that is, Big Business and Big Government. Which, of course, is exactly what happened.

It was Orestes Brownson who gave voice to the Yankees' grave misgivings about the Civil War. He wrote in his magazine, *Brownson's Quarterly Review*:

> We have some madmen amongst us who talk of exterminating the Southern leaders, and of New Englandizing the South. We wish to see the free-labor system substituted for the slave-labor system, but beyond that we have no wish to exchange or modify Southern society, and would rather approach Northern society to it, than it to Northern society.
>
> The New Englander has excellent points, but is restless in body and mind, always scheming, always in motion, never satisfied with what he has, and always seeking to make all the world like himself, or as uneasy as himself. He is smart, seldom great; educated, but seldom learned; active in mind, but rarely a profound thinker; religious, but thoroughly materialistic: his worship is rendered in a temple founded on Mammon, and he expects to be carried to heaven in a softly-cushioned railway car, with his sins carefully checked and deposited in the baggage crate with his other luggage to be duly delivered when he has reached his destination. He is philanthropic, but makes his philanthropy his excuse for meddling with everybody's business as if it were his own, and under pretense of

promoting religion and morality, he wars against every generous and natural instinct, and aggravates the very evils he seeks to cure.

Mind you, Orestes Brownson was born in Vermont to a respectable Puritan family. But he was a Northern Democrat like Pierce and Hawthorne, a Yankee Jeffersonian. The Federalists, Whigs, and Republicans in Boston were as alien to him as the Southern planters.

Eventually, Brownson (like Hawthorne) threw in his lot with the Union. But, like all New England countryfolk, he saw the Civil War as a lose-lose proposition. Regardless of whose army surrendered first, Winthrop's "model of charity" was crumbling before his eyes. Neither the North nor the South stood for that manly independence envisioned by John Smith. Abraham Lincoln was, at best, the devil they knew.

Hard as Reconstruction was for the South, Lincoln's triumph dealt a more severe blow to the North. At the onset of the war, Pierce gave a speech asking:

> What are to be the ultimate fruits of having first wronged and then conquered and humiliated a spirited and gallant people, whose fathers were the loved friends and co-laborers with our fathers in the Revolution, and who have nobly stood with us, as companions and fellow-soldiers, in every war with foreign foes since that period, remains to be seen.

The fruits were—as he predicted—the Boston commercial elite's teaming up with Washington's political elite to "modernize" the United States.

I wish it could go without saying that I don't believe the South was in the right during the Civil War. My own ancestors fought for the Union, and I'm proud of their service. But I wish, too, that we could acknowledge the unwanted and completely regrettable consequences that inevitably followed Abe Lincoln's victory.[1]

The glory of that victory was the abolition of chattel slavery. The tragedy was that, from then on, America ceased to be a commonwealth. It was no longer an association of freemen, bound together for the common defense. Forever after, membership in the United States was mandatory. To be called an *American* signified nothing more or less than the fact that one happened to be under the jurisdiction of Washington, D.C. The only "common wealth" was that based in the ports of Boston and the factories of Hartford; the "common defense" was the protection of those political elites and financial interests.

Still, I believe there's a way to reclaim the best of our American traditions. After all, traditions aren't just something you read about. They're a way of life. And nobody knew that better than that ancient Yankee, Robert Frost.

You know who that is, don't you? Sure you do. Everyone with a middle-school education has read "The Road Not Taken," whether he wanted to or not. Frost is *the* iconic American poet, the eternal laureate of New England. But not many people know that Frost's full name was Robert Lee Frost, after the famed Southern general. At the age of about fourteen, Frost's father ran away from his home in New Hampshire and tried to enlist in the Army of Northern Virginia.

Frost the Elder was what's known as a Copperhead, a Northern Democrat who sympathized with the Southern cause. But he never did join up with the Confederates. Some say he was captured by Union troops and sent back to his family. Others say the Rebels turned him away because he was too young. (The latter makes for a better story, I think, so that's the one I choose to believe.)

Frost the Younger remained a conservative and localist throughout the New Deal era. He called himself a Jeffersonian, and some of his fellow Democrats sometimes accused him of disloyalty to President Roosevelt. But he didn't care. If anything, he had a bit of fun playing the retrograde. So he wrote in his poem "Build Soil—A Political Pastoral":

> I was brought up
> A State-rights free-trade Democrat. What's that?
> An inconsistency.

In 1935, Frost attended a conference with Robert Penn Warren, regarded by many as the leader of the Southern Agrarians. The topic of the conference was Faulkner and the Southern novel, which didn't interest a Northerner like Frost in the slightest. But they did find a deeper kinship. Frost "had an interest in the Southern Agrarians," Warren reported, "and he called himself a Yankee Agrarian." Despite all the decades of bitter North–South acrimony, for these old agrarians it was like a family reunion—and, as with all family reunions, they found plenty to disagree about.

That's the America of the Puritan lawyer John Winthrop and the English soldier John Smith, of the Yankee John Adams and the Southerner Thomas Jefferson.

So, in that sense, America is a country where a true reactionary may feel the most at home. Not since the end of feudalism has any people achieved such a union of freedom and community, of federalism and localism acting as buffers against a national government. At bottom, we're still a nation of self-governing serfs. The spirit of the pilgrim, the pioneer, is integral to our national character. It keeps us humble, pious, and strong.

Americans feel a reflexive hatred of elitism that prevents us from getting too highbrow. But we also have a natural earnestness, an ingrained piety, that saves us from ever becoming really lowbrow. Like the culture of medieval Europe, American culture has always been firmly populist. It's accessible, in the way that good and true and beautiful things always are. As Tocqueville wrote in *Democracy in America*: "There is hardly a pioneer's hut which does not contain a few odd volumes of Shakespeare. I remember reading the feudal drama of *Henry V* for the first time in a log cabin."

Americans could admire the jousting, feasting, fighting, spitting, belching kings of the Middle Ages, perhaps even more so than dainty Europeans could. Mark Twain seemed to think so. There's a great line from *A Connecticut Yankee in King Arthur's Court* where he says, "The fact is, the king was a good deal more than a king, he was a man; and when a man is a man, you can't knock it out of him." Guys like Richard the Lionheart and Teddy Roosevelt would nod their heads vigorously. A dainty Bourbon prince would shrug and go back to his orgy.

And say the situations were reversed. Say you could take a knight, like Geoffroi de Charny—a man who lived and died by the code of chivalry—and bring him to Mark Twain's America. Would he hop a ship to France and carry water for Napoleon III? It's doubtful. I bet he'd sign on with the Rough Riders, or maybe head West and become a cowboy. As long as he could hear the Mass, he'd feel perfectly at home in the States.

So don't worry too much about Throne and Altar. As we've said all along, being a reactionary has very little to do with politics. Again, Tocqueville put it nicely: "The best laws cannot make a constitution work in spite of morals; morals can turn the worst laws to advantage."

Our countrymen have never waited for the government's permission to be free. We don't need politicians to tell us to love our neighbor. Charity and independence are like two birthmarks on the American soul, as they were on the medieval mind. They've marked us out from the beginning. They're the whole reason we exist. In America, every patriot is a reactionary, and so every reactionary ought to be a patriot.

CHAPTER TEN

Against Progress

Let us suffer absurdities, for that is only to suffer one another.

—Hilaire Belloc

To wrap up this historical section, let us conclude that except to the most debased hedonist, the most ardent skeptic, and the most ambitious oligarch, the Middle Ages must sound like a dream. Faith, reason, and imagination worked together in perfect accord. Culture was equally distributed among the classes, not hoarded by the elite. There was no tension between freedom and order. The law, as per New Testament and Catholic teaching, offered a "preferential option for the poor" by, among other means, protecting the rights of the serfs. Authority rested on the duty of the strong man to defend the weak. Today, we find it impossible to believe that such a society could ever exist. Except that it did.

So, why does the reactionary's neo-feudalism strike so many as absurd? Why is it that, having cut through all the anti-medieval propaganda peddled by professional historians, the very phrase "neo-feudalism" makes many roll their eyes? The answer comes from the near universal embrace of the Whig version of history, which holds that the past is nothing more than an inevitable march towards our liberal, democratic modernity.

The great Catholic historian Christopher Dawson observed that "every period of civilization possesses certain characteristic ideas that are peculiarly its own." Yet, "so long as they are dominant, their unique and original character is never fully recognized, since they are accepted as principles of absolute truth and universal validity. They are looked on not as popular ideas of the moment, but as eternal truths implanted in the very nature of things, and as self-evident in any kind of rational thinking."

For our own civilization, Dawson argues, that characteristic idea is progress: "the belief that every day and in every way the world grows better and better." This dogma of progress will serve as the primary antagonist of this little book. For progress, as our contemporaries use the word, is retrospective. We begin with the assumption that we "moderns" believe all the right sorts of things, and that the process that led to our believing them was therefore good and proper. History is only the long, agonizing slog through prejudice and superstition culminating in our magnificent modernity. Progress, then, is simply the means by which we acquired IKEA furniture, McDonald's hamburgers, and the Department of Education. Who could possibly say otherwise?

Of course, the progressive is usually more subtle than that. He may resent the rise of fast food; he may lament the decline of craftsmanship; he may occasionally cast a wary glance over the growing nanny state. Yet he insists that these are necessary trade-offs for the many real advances that have occurred in our society since we banished all those grim, medieval superstitions. Could we have achieved universal suffrage without the Reign of Terror? Could we have discovered penicillin without marginalizing the Catholic Church?

For the progressive, the answer is a resounding *No*.

That's because his worldview is fundamentally Whiggish. The dogma of progress has so conditioned his mind that he can't imagine the world any other way. The blessings of modernity must be accepted meekly along with its scourges, for we are all merely actors playing our assigned roles in the ineluctable unfolding drama of progress.

Lord Tennyson accidentally gave voice to liberal fatalism when he wrote, "Let the great world spin for ever down the ringing grooves of change." We do not chart our own course; we merely roll down a groove, like a marble circling the drain.

A reactionary is born every time a Westerner recognizes how entrenched the dogma of progress has become in our civilization. By recognizing the progressive spell, he breaks it. That's why the reactionary is the only true freethinker. He's free to imagine a better future and to remember the better past. He's able to learn at the feet of those dead masters who found themselves on the "wrong side of history"—which is, more often than not, the right side of eternity.

"But you can't turn back the clock!" the progressive howls. "Nonsense," says the reactionary. "Just pull out the pin and spin it the other way. Here, like this. Pretend you're adjusting your watch for daylight savings, give or take about six centuries." How far back do we turn the clock? Seven hundred years, if we're ambitious—or, in America, two hundred will do, in a pinch.

PART II

This Is Now

CHAPTER ELEVEN

Among the Champagne Socialists

There is no weaker nation than the one in which every
citizen is rich.
—Louis de Bonald

I think our old comrade Friederich Engels would have felt perfectly at home in modern America. Referred to by his son-in-law as "the great beheader of champagne bottles," Engels was born to a family of prosperous German mill owners. He was the perfect and consummate hypocrite. Engels spent his days calling for the proletariat to rise up against their capitalist overlords; at night, he invited those same overlords over to sup on his famous lobster salad. To Karl Marx himself, he once remarked: "If I had an income of 5,000 francs I would do nothing but work and amuse myself with women until I went to pieces. If there were no Frenchwomen, life wouldn't be worth living. But so long as there are grisettes, well and good!"

Engels wanted to raise the proletariat to the level of the bourgeoisie—and isn't that what America has done? Whether we like it or not, our consumer culture, our successful capitalism, our massive government-academic-corporate-media superstructure pushing "diversity, inclusion, and equity" have given us a society where we're all champagne socialists now.

We get an impression of Engels as a gross old pervert. Today, you'd find him teaching at Harvard, lecturing about women's equality and flirting with the coeds. I'm sure you've met someone of his ilk, and I'm sure you've also been struck by the fact that lechers are, to a man, insufferably boring.

The same is true of America's Engelian society. Irving Kristol once said that a "bourgeois civilization" such as America's is

> uninterested in such transcendence, which it at best toler-ates as a private affair, a matter of individual taste and individual consumption, as it were. It is prosaic, not only in form but in essence. It is a society organized for the convenience and comfort of common men and women, not for the production of heroic, memorable figures. It is a society interested in making the best of this world, not in any kind of transfiguration, whether through tragedy or piety.

Peter Viereck made the same observation in *Conservatism Revisited*, calling the modern bourgeois "unhappy and untragic." It's painfully apt.

So what do Americans do? They work—and yet survey after survey shows that most Americans don't like their jobs.

Job satisfaction is usually tied to income. In a way, of course, that makes sense. In another way, it shows that most Americans are resigned to working only as a source of income. Only some reckless dreamer (an artist, for instance, or a nurse) would be willing to chase a career he loves, that gives his life meaning, even if it means bringing home a smaller paycheck.

We spend at least forty hours a week at our jobs, and yet the thought that we should enjoy those hours strikes us as fanciful. As long as we can afford to lease a new Explorer and spend a week in Mexico every year, we're satisfied.

The average workday is eight hours; on top of that, the average worker spends about an hour commuting to and from work. Assuming one sleeps for eight hours, this leaves seven hours of leisure. Assume that one also spends an hour getting ready for work and another hour cooking and cleaning afterwards. That leaves five hours. How do we spend them?

A 2018 Nielsen report found that American adults waste eleven hours per day consuming media—much of it, presumably, on the clock. But that includes four hours of television. It's by no means uncommon for a man to come home from work, watch TV until bedtime, sleep, get up the next morning, go to work, and then start all over again. What kind of life is that? The answer is, "No kind of life at all." Small wonder, then, that one in ten Americans is on anti-depressants, that our country is suffering an opioid addiction epidemic, and that suicide rates are skyrocketing (especially among young people, whose media consumption is even greater).

In fact, when we take the long view of history, we can see how much of our culture's fascination with the perverse and the abnormal stems from the sheer tedium of modern life. Each year, more and more young people identify as lesbian, gay, bisexual, or transgender. Is that because our society only recently allowed gay toddlers to "live out loud"? Or is it because our culture automatically assumes that homosexuals or bisexuals or any variety of other-than-monogamous-heterosexuals are more interesting and more admirable and more liberated? How many little girls wear chest binders and get bowl cuts just so they can stand out—or, rather, so they can fit in with our "LGBT-affirming" culture?

As Margaret Mead once said, "Always remember that you are absolutely unique. Just like everyone else."

The first step towards restoring a real civilization in the West is to put this shallow, rotten, bourgeois culture out of its misery. The reactionary is a partisan of tragedy, of piety, of happiness. He, and only he, is willing to stand against the dictatorship of comfort and convenience.

Today, every Christian has a duty to join his ranks. "For what is the Pharisee," asked Christopher Dawson,

> but a spiritual bourgeois, a typically "closed" nature, a man who applies the principle of calculation and gain not to economics but to religion itself, a hoarder of merits, who reckons his accounts with heaven as though God was his banker? It is against this "closed," self-sufficient moralist ethic that the fiercest denunciations of the Gospels are directed. Even the sinner who possesses a seed of generosity, a faculty of self-surrender, and an openness of spirit is nearer to the kingdom of heaven than the "righteous" Pharisee; for the soul that is closed to love is closed to grace.

That isn't to say that every middle-class person is a Pharisee, of course. On the contrary. Given how endemic depression, anxiety, addiction, and suicide have become in our society, there seem to be a great many people whose souls are revolting against our bourgeois culture.

As in the time of Christ, the true Pharisees comprise a small political and financial elite. They uphold the champagne socialist system because it serves their interests. They go by names such as Jeff Bezos, Hillary Clinton, Bill Gates, and Mike Bloomberg. They tell us that the past was bad and they are the future, that the future will be one of ever greater convenience and comfort, and that there is no alternative but a return to racism and sexism and inequality. The "conservatives" who seek to "conserve" this status quo are merely their useful idiots.

The great evil of progressivism is that by denigrating the past it raises ingratitude to a virtue and blinds us to the lessons of experience. The great evil of conservatism today is that it is willing to surrender the past as long as markets are "free." Conservatives can then join liberals in praising progress. But is it really "progress" in any worthwhile sense?

The point of the past is not to dwell upon it, but to take eternal truths from it and return them to the present, where they have been misplaced—or suppressed. Dawson, as usual, put it best: "It may even be questioned, as indeed it has been questioned by many, whether the modern advance of Western civilization is progress in the true sense of the word; whether men are happier or wiser or better than they were in simpler states of society, and whether [twentieth-century] Birmingham or Chicago is to be preferred to Medieval Florence."

The reactionary's role is to return life to its natural rhythms and eternal truths, free the slaves of comfort, rescue the victims of convenience, and do what conservatives are incapable of doing: point out the path to an older, better way, a way of self-sufficiency, independence, and freedom, far away from the champagne socialists and their coercive, deadening bourgeois dystopia.

CHAPTER TWELVE

A Humane Economy: The View from Nazareth

Then the Gods of the Market tumbled,
and their smooth-tongued wizards withdrew,
And the hearts of the meanest were humbled
and began to believe it was true
That All is not Gold that Glitters,
and Two and Two make Four—
And the Gods of the Copybook Headings
limped up to explain it once more.
—Rudyard Kipling

Once upon a time, if a man wanted to live on the coast of Maine, he had to be at the docks by four o'clock in the morning to find a job on a lobster boat. If he wanted to live on a few dozen acres in Virginia, he had to buy a farm and get up at four o'clock in the morning to milk the cows. If he wanted a ranch in Wyoming, he had to learn how to ride and wrangle horses and shoot mountain lions.

These weren't easy lives, to be sure. But we could do it. You could; I could. Because human beings have been doing it for thousands of years. That was the deal. God appointed Adam as the steward of his creation, and stewardship is hard work. It's good, meaningful work.

But it's hard. And the Boss expects a return on his investment, as in the parable of the talents from Matthew's Gospel. God wants us to make something of ourselves. He wants us to do the kind of work we were made for, and to do it well.

When I was a kid in rural Massachusetts, I worked on a neighbor's farm. And I loved it. It was the best job I ever had, and probably the best job I ever will have. My parents scrimped and saved to send me to a good prep school, but I didn't want to go to college. I wanted to be a farmer. I begged my dad to let me transfer to the local agricultural and technical school, but he said no. "Where are you going to get the money to buy a farm?" And, hey! He was right. It's expensive to be a peasant these days.

I was born in Newburyport. My family's earliest ancestor we could find, Jeremiah Travis, lived there in the 1600s. Our family belongs to a group called "Swamp Yankees," which are like poor WASPs. Go outside the big New England cities and you'll find farmers and fishermen with names like Cabot, Lowell, Bush, Dudley, Emerson, Lodge, Forbes, and Sears. They're distant cousins of the Boston Brahmin, such as George Bush and William Weld, but our ancestors never made it big. On the census, these families give their ethnicity as "American" because they've been here so long they can't remember being anything else.

When I came of age, I used to go down to a pub by the docks in Newburyport and drink with the fishermen. Most of their families had lived in town since the colonial era, but for many of them gentrification was making their way of life unaffordable. All around me Swamp Yankees are being displaced from the land and the sea they've worked for centuries. And some idiot millennial might grin and say, "Serves them right for what they did to the Indians," because this is the brave, new world we live in now, where no one cares about the past or tradition except to say that they were bad. The coast of Maine, the plains of Wyoming, and the Virginia countryside are being bought up—often by wealthy vacationers who have no interest in nature except for the pretty views. And, man, are the views ever pretty. But that's not what nature is *for*. It's not an ornament for some rich guy to put in his curio cabinet like a Fabergé egg.

We pooh-pooh Thomas Jefferson's idea that the "yeoman farmer" is the backbone of our republic. I have my own reservations about Jefferson, but on this point he was exactly right. America is more than a body politic. It's more than a random assortment of individuals who happen to be ruled by the same Beltway bureaucrats. America is a *place*; Americans are a *people*. More precisely, America is a union of many places and peoples who've decided to bind themselves to one another in a commonwealth, providing for a common defense and striving for a common destiny.

And community is about dependence. We depend on our people and our place, or else we don't have a community. If the Atlantic is just some body of water that a New York financier likes to look at for three weeks in the summer, he can't belong to the place that is Maine. He can't belong to the people we call Mainers. He doesn't need the sea or the seafarers, and they don't need him. If anything, they're better off without his driving up their property taxes.

Of course, it's not solely the fault of the rich. Another line of the Davis family came from Prince Edward Island. They were subsistence fishermen. My grandmother remembers visiting her kin in their shack on the ocean—the most gorgeous piece of coastal land in Canada— where they lived in total destitution. They couldn't read or write. They stored their perishables in a bucket, which they lowered into the well to keep them cold. One year, they got a new "lamp"—a single light-bulb suspended from the ceiling of their shanty.

The next year, she went back and found three huge McMansions being built between their shack and the water. They'd sold their view to a developer, for what I'm sure they thought was a lot of money—maybe enough to buy a second lightbulb. I don't know what came of them, but I'm sure their kids left Prince Edward Island as soon as they could hop the ferry.

So, is this a question of city slickers exploiting white trash? Or is it a matter of greedy Swamp Yankees selling out their inheritance for pocket money? I don't see that it matters. The point is that once these communities and lifestyles die, they never come back. My Canadian kinfolk—whether they're working as baristas in Ottawa or collecting welfare in Winnipeg—probably have no idea that, had life turned out a little differently, they could've been fishermen sitting on a $3 million piece of property on the coast.

Now, maybe they wouldn't *want* to be fishermen. My point is that, now, they *couldn't* be. They'd be met with the same conundrum I was. "Where are you going to get the money for a boat? Where are you going to learn how to fish commercially? Why would any able seaman want to join your crew?"

Once Swamp Yankees are displaced, they generally don't flourish. My own ancestors went to work in the shoe mills of Lawrence and Lowell, Massachusetts, until the mills closed and their jobs were shipped overseas; then they got jobs with the municipal government as police officers and firefighters. But plenty of other Swamp Yankees didn't fare so well. They wound up in redneck reservations like the ones described by J. D. Vance in *Hillbilly Elegy*.

I talk about the Swamp Yankees because it's the world I know. But the same is happening everywhere. In September 2019, *The Atlantic* reported on how banks, developers, and agribusinesses were taking over agriculture in Georgia, pricing black farmers off land their families had received as land grants from the Freedmen's Bureau after the Civil War. Agribusiness might be more efficient than family farms, but the real question is: efficient *for whom?* These black families are no longer yeoman farmers. Are they better off in gentrifying Atlanta, or will they have to sell out there, too? Where is their place in this world?

As a wise man once said, "Man shall not live by bread alone." That is why economics is a pseudo-science. To think about human beings merely as consumers and producers is a category error. The economist is only interested in the relative value of *stuff*. And yet, this kind of impoverished idea of "value" has infected every aspect of public life. We act as though capital and goods—mere stuff—are the only things we can talk about as having any "objective" worth.

Conservatives who champion neoliberalism or the Austrian School or any other such economic theory are no different than the Marxists who take a purely materialist view of human nature. Economics as we know it is a product of the Enlightenment; it can't speak to the view that man is a creature made in God's image and likeness. Seventy percent of Americans identify as Christian. Only 3 percent are atheists—total, convinced materialists. Yet every conversation we have about economics is supposed to tailor itself to that 3 percent. Every great religious and philosophical tradition, almost without exception, claims that an excess of wealth is detrimental to human well-being. Everyone—from Socrates to Marcus Aurelius, from the Buddha to Jesus Christ—has argued that human happiness lies in simple living and detachment from worldly desires. Yet somehow, in our modern materialist prejudices, "economics" has taken priority.

Early in the twentieth century, a group of men and women recognized this problem and began working out a new mode of economic thinking called distributism. It was supposed to be an alternative to both capitalism and socialism—one that really did act as though man were made in God's image and likeness. It tried to account for his higher, spiritual needs as well as his lower, material ones.

The best-known leaders of this movement were our English friends G. K. Chesterton and Hilaire Belloc. The torch was carried in the United States by journalists such as Herbert Agar and activists such as Dorothy Day. My favorite distributist writer, though, was a Dominican friar named Vincent McNabb.

In explaining the distributist vision, Father McNabb pointed to "The Call of Nazareth":

> For us, Nazareth was always a highland hamlet, whose every stone was hallowed by thirty years of God's redemptive love. Gradually our eyes began to see this highland hamlet as one of the necessities...of the enterprise of Redemption. For Nazareth was the Unit of human society. It was a family of families gathered together in aid and defense of life. Within its circuit dwelt the little self-sufficing group of land-workers and hand-workers.

Theologians talk about "the scandal of the Incarnation," but rarely do they talk about the kind of society that God chose to be incarnated *in*. That's the real scandal. Imagine: He elected to be born in this small town on the margins of the Roman Empire. His stepfather was a carpenter, and Jesus worked in Joseph's shop for the first thirty years of his life—a robust middle age by the standards of the day. He was an "essential worker" in a community where *every* worker was essential. Nazareth wasn't a thriving metropolis like Jerusalem or a royal city like Bethlehem. It was so modest that Bartholomew the Apostle asked, "Can anything good come out of Nazareth?"

Most of Jesus's neighbors, customers, and kinfolk (they were all the same people) would have been farmers. And here, again, Father McNabb makes an interesting observation:

The Word made flesh was not minded to disturb the Divine order which made land-work the primary duty and need of beings demanding daily bread to keep them in being. It was only from the work of secondary need such as fishing or of still less need such as tax-collecting that Jesus chose his disciples. Land-work was an institution so indispensable and divine that from it he took no workers, but only the wisdom of parables.

John Crowe Ransom belonged to that clique of twentieth-century American writers called the Twelve Southerners, or the Southern Agrarians. Most of their writings focused more on the cultural and moral virtues of the traditional agrarian society. But Ransom was also a trenchant, McNabbian critic of industrial capitalism. At the heart of his manifesto *Land!* is an observation equally simple and profound: men can't eat metal.

The steel maker makes steel, or at least some part of it, but he cannot eat steel, nor clothe himself with it, nor shelter under it from the rain; there being no direct connection between his own act of manufacture and what he needs in order to live. The farmer, on the other hand, is engaged in producing vegetables, meats, tobacco, fibers, timber—precisely the raw materials of the staples of living, and some of them ready for immediate consumption. The steel man must get money. The farmer may get money if he likes; but he may also prefer to provide himself with his necessities with hardly the exchange of a dollar. Nobody else in the whole economic society is in that position.

No less than Stuart Chase, the architect of the New Deal, credited the amphibian farmer with seeing America through the Depression. "When the books won't balance," Chase observed, "he has only to throw them out the window and go pick some peas." According to the Bureau of Labor Statistics, in 2019 a total of 1.9 percent of the U.S. workforce was employed in agriculture, forestry, fishing, and hunting. Just 0.5 percent were self-employed farmers. Right before the Depression, about 20 percent of Americans were employed in agriculture. By 1933, about 25 percent of employed Americans were farmers of one sort or another. Throughout the Depression, the agricultural sector made small gains while gross unemployment elsewhere skyrocketed.

The coronavirus pandemic brought America to the very brink of a second Great Depression. As it stands, grocery stores in our major cities stock about enough food to last three days. If the supply chain were ever to break down—as it very nearly did last year—people in New York City would begin starving in the first week. I know you love your iPhones and Nike Airs, but if the going gets tough—and it will—you can't eat them.

Unfortunately, America's agricultural output has been "capitalized": turned over to cash crops like maize and soybeans. There's very little demand for these crops as food—most Americans don't eat corn and tofu at every meal—but they are heavily subsidized by the U.S. government. For whatever reason, we use tax dollars to pay farmers to grow them. Yet, because we pay good money for these worthless foodstuffs, we've had to artificially engineer demand to keep up with the inflated supply. That's why everything is now sweetened with high-fructose corn syrup, despite the fact that sugar is healthier and tastes a whole lot better.

So, if another Depression *did* hit America, the few remaining farmers wouldn't even be able to live off their own crops, let alone share their surplus with their neighbors. They'd have hundreds of acres of arable land, and yet they'd die of malnutrition within months, their bodies bloated from all the corn and their testicles withered from all the soy. If we were governed by statesmen, and if our economy made sense, you would think someone would notice this and encourage us to do something about it.

The COVID-19 pandemic exposed another fundamental problem with our economy: most Americans don't make things. Most of us are *unessential* workers; our *value* to the economy is as *consumers*. During the pandemic we could stay home and send emails and do Zoom calls and the government could send us COVID checks to spend at Amazon. This is "consumer capitalism" for the twenty-first century.

Now I refer you to an essay by anthropologist David Graeber titled "On the Phenomenon of Bullshit Jobs." In it, Mr. Graeber writes:

> In the year 1930, John Maynard Keynes predicted that, by century's end, technology would have advanced sufficiently that countries like Great Britain or the United States would have achieved a 15-hour work week. There's every reason to believe he was right. In technological terms, we are quite capable of this. And yet it didn't happen. Instead, technology has been marshaled, if anything, to figure out ways to make us all work more. In order to achieve this, jobs have had to be created that are, effectively, pointless. Huge swathes of people, in Europe and North America in particular, spend their entire working lives performing tasks they secretly believe do not really need to be performed. The moral and spiritual damage that comes from this situation is profound. It is a scar across our collective soul. Yet virtually no one talks about it....

The service industry accounts for about 80 percent of the U.S. workforce. Retail, leisure, and hospitality alone account for a whopping 20 percent. Another 13 percent work in "professional and business services." For comparison, the entire goods-producing sector—agriculture, manufacturing, mining, and construction—accounts for about 14 percent, total. How could this house of cards not come crashing down?

Here's another thing: if you get in the habit of paying folks to stay home watching Netflix and shopping on Amazon, you're going to have a hard time convincing them to go back to their bullshit jobs. Once they realize they're unessential workers, they're going to stop working. Because they don't have to. Their work isn't necessary.

This is why Andrew Yang is the most important politician of our time. He sparked the first real conversation about a universal basic income. A universal basic income (or UBI) is a stipend that would be paid to every citizen in the country merely for existing. Mr. Yang would begin by paying every American $1,000 per month. Mr. Yang's UBI almost matches the federal minimum wage. Under his scheme, a married couple could support one child—without either spouse's working—and still remain above the poverty line.

Mr. Yang's proposal seems fanciful, but it's not. It's inevitable. A UBI is a redundancy package for the American worker. The only question is: Would such an outcome really be desirable? Is the abolition of work a good thing? As usual, Wendell Berry put it best:

> The great question that hovers over this issue, one that we have dealt with mainly by indifference, is the question of what people are *for*. Is their greatest dignity in unemployment? Is the obsolescence of human beings now our social goal? One would conclude so from our attitude toward work, especially the manual work necessary to the

long-term preservation of the land, and from our rush toward mechanization, automation, and computerization. In a country that puts an absolute premium on labor-saving measures, short workdays, and retirement, why should there be any surprise at permanence of unemployment and welfare dependency? Those are only different names for our national ambition.

Mr. Yang and his followers will find no real opposition from free-market conservatives. They won't be able to convince the American people that workfare is somehow preferable to welfare, that meaning-less employment is better than gainful unemployment. They won't scare people with talk about Big Government because Big Government and Big Business are in alliance to "help" consumers. For most Americans, a big government that sends people checks to watch Netflix and shop at Amazon isn't a problem. It's a solution (if a bad one) to the real problems of wage slavery, bullshit jobs, and a quality of life measurably worse than that of a medieval serf.

American conservatives, however, are finally getting worried that progressive Big Business will begin cutting off right-of-center customers from the economy. PayPal is refusing to serve anyone it designates as a "white nationalist," which will soon include everyone to the right of President Kamala Harris. The insurance company AIG allegedly canceled the policy of Curt Schilling, a former baseball player, because it disapproved of his pro-Trump tweets. Back in 2014, Mozilla co-founder and CEO Brendan Eich was ousted from his own company for donating to Proposition 8, which defended traditional marriage in California. Donald Trump, the former president of the United States, for crying out loud, has been banned from social media, and banks and other organizations have said they won't do business with him.

Here's the reality: America, with conservatives' blessing, has become utterly dependent on big corporations. We rely on the global supply chain and its left-wing gatekeepers for everything from food to clothes to medicine. Hell, the United States imports more than $7 billion in fertilizer each year. And globalism's progressive masters have every right to turn off the tap if they so choose. We have what Henry George referred to as "virtual slavery under the forms of freedom"; we are utterly dependent on Big Business and Big Government.

Really, conservatism became redundant the day it threw its lot in with Henry Ford. That was the real, prophetic genius of Aldous Huxley in his book *Brave New World*. He saw that Fordism was only a stepping-stone to the total welfare state. It would make human beings obsolete. And once humans were obsolete, the powers that be would herd them like cattle. Work kept man happy; labor kept him occupied; soma keeps him stupid and pliant. Netflix and Amazon are our soma. And President Yang will write us a check so we can have as much as we like.

Until about a year ago, the mainstream Right was gung ho about Big Business. And, of course, the mainstream Left has always been pretty gung ho about Big Government. Yet, Big Business and Big Government have been best friends since childhood—at least since the Dissolution of the Monasteries and the arrival of the New Men. In this sense, the Left and the Right acted as the two arms of centralization, drawing all wealth and power into the hands of a small, well-connected, super-affluent elite.

Once again, Wendell Berry put it best: "As a social or economic goal, bigness is totalitarian; it establishes an inevitable tendency towards the *one* that will be the biggest of all." Now, that "one" might be efficient. It could micromanage every aspect of public life, both political and economic. I doubt it. But it will certainly try.

Until just a few years ago, most conservatives thought this process of centralization was inevitable. More than that, they called it "progress." The destruction of local communities and economies was defended in the name of efficiency. The men who destroyed them were called entrepreneurs and venture capitalists. They dismantled family farms and shipped factories overseas. They were hailed as "job creators" when those farmers and laborers took jobs stocking shelves at Walmart or making frappuccinos at Starbucks.

The reactionary understands that Big Government and Big Business are both enemies of freedom, and that to fight both, we have to rethink what our economy is *for*. We know that real progress can only begin when mankind is ready to answer the call of Nazareth, to return to a life of neighborliness, to a life of small farms and small businesses in real community, to an economy built on a human scale where every job is essential.

And that begins by recognizing that our economy should be *for families*.

Margaret Thatcher was almost right when she said, "There's no such thing as society. There are individual men and women and there are families." Actually, there are *only* families.

Even if a man doesn't have a wife and children, he has a mother and a father. They are his first teachers, his first governors, his first countrymen; it is in the home that we learn our first economy. It is in the home that the most important of all jobs is done—the raising of the next generation.

And that's why it is imperative that we get women out of the workforce.

Now, don't misunderstand me. I don't mean the poor Fantines who need to support their children. But women's (wholly unnecessary) entrance into the labor force in the early twentieth century was a disaster.

Don't take my word for it, though. In her excellent 2003 book *The Two-Income Trap*, Senatrix Elizabeth Warren notes:

> When millions of mothers entered the workforce, they ratcheted up the price of a middle-class life for everyone, including families that wanted to keep Mom at home. A generation ago, a single breadwinner who worked diligently and spent carefully could assure his family a comfortable position in the middle class. But the frenzied bidding war, fueled by families with two incomes, changed the game for single-income families as well, pushing them down the economic ladder.

How could it be otherwise?

When women first began to seek employment outside the home, they were called "pin-money workers." They got jobs not because they needed to support themselves or their families, but because they wanted a little extra spending money for hat pins and whatnot. Slowly, however, these women workers created a severe labor surplus. Where three men had once competed for a single job, suddenly two women were added to the mixture. This deflated the value of labor, depressing wages. But even if women didn't earn as much as men, a two-income household might have (say) 1.5 times the spending power of a single-income household. That additional spending power meant prices increased so that even as real wages were deflating, the cost of living went up—enough to render the husband-as-breadwinner model virtually untenable. It was a robber baron's dream. He could charge his customers more *and* pay his employees less.

In the 1930s, the average cost of a new home was slightly less than half an average worker's income. In the 1960s, it was a little *over* half.

By the 1980s, it had shot up to three and a half times the average income. Today, it's five or six times higher.

As an aside, I'll add that, before we began consolidating all the family farms—before we moved all the craftsmen out of their workshops and onto the assembly line—women *did* have a role to play "in the workplace." They worked alongside their husbands—and also did the cooking, the cleaning, and the lion's share of the child-rearing.

And that's good! That's normal. That's work worth doing. The problem with the modern economy *isn't* that women work (in the Middle Ages women certainly worked, including as doctors). It's that the *kind* of work they do is antithetical to family life.

Then again, that's true of men as well. Fathers who kept their own workshop—who owned the means of their (modest) production—could pop upstairs when they needed to do their paternal duties. Likewise, the farmer's wife could milk the cows or churn butter when she wasn't busy with the children. Today, working women, like working men, are forced to be part-time parents.

Why women chose to re-enter the workforce only to slave away in sweatshops and cramped offices, I can't say. As Chesterton said, feminism "is mixed up with a muddled idea that women are free when they serve their employers but slaves when they help their husbands."

Here's another great line: "There have been household gods and household saints and household fairies. I am not sure that there have yet been any factory gods or factory saints or factory fairies." Women just don't belong in these places. And neither do men.

Anyway, the great tragedy of it all is that many moms don't *want* to work outside the home but feel they must. In 2019, a Gallup poll found that 50 percent of women with children under the age of eighteen wanted to be homemakers. The problem is that most of them can't. Their husbands' wages are too low, and the cost of living is too high.

The early critics of feminism warned that this exact scenario would play itself out if women kept seeking "independence" from the home by selling themselves into corporate slavery. Writing in the distributist magazine *Free America* back in 1937, Mrs. Ralph Borsodi pleaded with her sex to ignore the noisome propaganda about "empowerment" and consider the more fundamental question:

> What concerns me most is the question of what is a good way for the average woman to live. I do not believe that spending the best part of her life in a cannery, a textile mill, a garment factory, a power laundry, nor even behind the counters of a department store or sitting behind a typewriter, is as good a way to live as most of the defenders of industrialism and socialism seem to believe. For the average woman, it seems to me that running a home, taking care of and training her children, and doing creative work—as crafts like sewing and weaving as well as cooking and washing—is a better way of living....
>
> I don't want the millions of women who have chosen homemaking as a career to think they are producing less than the women who earn a little cash each week. And above all, I don't want those who are choosing their lifework to feel that they must abandon the country for the city, postpone marriage until they are too old to adjust to it, and give up the idea of establishing a family, because "progress" requires that they live in city flats, take city jobs, and spend their time in city shopping.

I'm not the least bit concerned with yanking all women out of the office and chaining them to the dishwasher. My concern is only for the 50 percent of women with young children who want to spend more time with their kids. I suspect that number would increase propitiously if it were considered a realistic option. In many neighborhoods populated by single mothers or "empowered" working women, it's probably considered the unlikeliest alternative lifestyle of all.

In May 2020—just two months into COVIDtide, when schools began closing en masse—40 percent of parents said they were more likely to homeschool their kids once the pandemic was over. Apparently, 40 percent of parents discovered that they actually enjoyed having their kids around and thought they could teach them better than public school teachers. (I bet a lot of kids secretly enjoyed being able to spend more time with their families, too. Families enjoy being together. What a concept.) More recent studies show that African American families are especially interested in homeschooling. Likewise, I expect that number would be higher if moms weren't both working full-time from home and teaching their kids.

Capitalists and socialists both promise ever-greater economic freedom. But let me ask you this: How are they going to free up those young mothers so they can stay home with the tykes? If they can't answer that question, any talk of "reform" is just wind. If we can't restore financial self-determination to American families, we can't hope to build a republic of charity.

As before, the problem is with the nature of our work.

Democrats are forever trying to raise the minimum wage, while Republicans are forever complaining that doing so would put low-skill workers out of a job. But again, Democrats and Republicans are united in focusing on the wrong thing. What we should support is a family wage. We should insist that every man be able to earn enough to support his wife and children at home without mom's having to work. Before women entered the workforce, the family wage was a standard American business model.

After all, that's what jobs are for (as we once understood)—to support a family. They don't exist to earn profits for corporate shareholders. They exist to help normal people earn a living. People don't exist to serve economies; economies exist to serve people. If the economy can't provide each breadwinner with a decent wage, the answer isn't to force women into the workforce, or for men and women to defer marriage indefinitely. The answer is to fix the economy.

It's really not that complicated. Haven't you ever wondered why your grandparents had a much nicer house than you do? Or how they bought it when they were half your age? Or how they filled it with sturdy wooden furniture? Have you ever wondered why your grandmother never had to work, even with five kids, but you and your husband work two jobs just to keep your dog in kibble? Our GDP continues to grow, but most of that wealth is going to plutocrats (such as the ones who control Big Tech). Real wages are falling as the cost of living rises.

According to a 2020 report by the *Washington Post*, millennials own 4 percent of real estate value in the United States. Baby Boomers, at the same age, owned 32 percent. In 2019, the Federal Reserve published a study showing that millennials own just 3 percent of all wealth in this country. Baby Boomers, at the same age, owned 21 percent. There's nothing wrong with a little inequality, of course, but to call this propitious decline in relative wealth "progress" is just insane.

Socialism looks to regulate the economy to ensure that it is run efficiently and scientifically, with its spoils divided evenly, while being indifferent or even hostile to families (socialists think in terms of "workers"). Consumer capitalism starts with an economy as society's building block and then tries to find a place for the family (as a body of consumers). Reactionaries take the family as a "given" and then build an economy around it, as in the Nazareth of Jesus's time.

Would gross domestic product fall on the reactionary model? Maybe, but that's okay. The Big Tech oligarchs don't need more money; American workers and families do. The return of the family wage is one way to do that; another is to bring back jobs that have been sent overseas. That means putting up aggressive tariffs and giving tax breaks to companies that repatriate jobs to America.

Whatever his faults, President Trump helped us to realize that the Republican Party's commitment to free-market economics was destroying the small communities that have always served as a bastion of traditional values, strong families, and religious faith. Conservatives were eating their own in the name of corporate profits and gross domestic product. The return of protectionism to the Republican Party was welcome, because putting America first is a necessary first step to putting our families first. Faith, hope, and charity begin at home. Home—the family—should be the focal point of our economy as well.

CHAPTER THIRTEEN

All News Is Fake News

Read not the Times. Read the Eternities.
—Henry David Thoreau

The patron saint of journalists is Saint Francis de Sales—a man who never wrote a newspaper column in his life. In fact, de Sales died in the year 1622. The first-ever weekly newspaper was founded just seventeen years earlier. Its German publishers, in all their glorious Germanic efficiency, gave it the name *Relation aller Fürnemmen und gedenckwürdigen Historien*, or "Account of All Distinguished and Memorable Stories."

As it happens, no journalist has ever been canonized in the roughly 2,020 years of Christian history. There have been thieves (Dismas), prostitutes (Mary of Egypt), ex-Satanists (Bartolo Longo), and even politicians (Thomas More). There's a movement afoot to canonize Jacques Fesch, a French cop-killer who became a devout Catholic in prison while awaiting execution. And yet not a single journalist. Apparently, Holy Mother Church doesn't think very highly of journalists—and surely with good reason.

G. K. Chesterton was supposed to be the first sainted scribbler, until an English bishop quashed his cause because his writings allegedly contain anti-Semitic sentiments. It's rather an odd charge to bring against a man who, on witnessing the rise of Nazi Germany, declared that he would "die defending the last Jew in Europe." Still, it goes to show: anyone who publishes his thoughts for a living will inevitably write something objectionable.

The first bit of advice I give would-be journalists is that no one really cares what we think. We are popular only insofar as we please an audience that already agrees with us. The journalist is the mirror of ignorance: the public comes to a conclusion and the journalist provides the "proof." That is all.

So journalists choose sides—and the only time a journalist crosses the aisle is when it's good for his career. Take Max Boot.

Mr. Boot was once a doyen of neoconservative foreign-policy circles, and one who made much of his "advising" Republican presidential candidates. After he emerged as a fanatical opponent of Donald Trump during the 2016 election, the left-wing *Washington Post* offered Mr. Boot a column. (The few token "conservative" columnists at the *Washington Post* and the *New York Times* were almost uniformly Never-Trumpers.) Boot had no qualms about denouncing his former colleagues and renouncing the mantle of conservatism (which, as a social liberal, had never quite suited him anyway).

What's the going rate for a journalist's soul? I can't say for sure, but a *New York* magazine article from the year 2000 says that columnists at our major newspapers earn between $150,000 and $350,000. So, somewhere in that range, most likely.

I stumbled into this profession and make less than $60,000 per year, but $350,000 just to tell people what they want to hear? Not a bad gig.

Journalists are the intelligentsia for an anti-intellectual age. When men haven't the patience to read books, they read newspapers. When they're too stupid to form ideas, they form opinions. Having read a good many newspapers, they eventually feel entitled to impose their opinions on the whole country. That's when they go to vote.

The first great American newspaper columnist was H. L. Mencken. He was an atheist, a racist, an anti-Semite, and a devotee of Nietzsche. He mocked every American who didn't share his contempt for religion, democracy, and the fairer sex—and was terrifically funny about it. He realized that newspapers sold entertainment—and he entertained at a high level.

If Mencken was America's most important columnist, William F. Buckley Jr. runs a close second. Like Mencken, he embraced his role as a showman. Unlike Mencken, he used his status as a public wit to sway the electorate.

And I don't mean with the magazine he founded, *National Review*, which always had a small circulation and takes itself too seriously to serve even as "newstainment." The only reason Buckley remains relevant is because all the episodes of his television show, *Firing Line*, are free to watch on YouTube. And it was *Firing Line* that made William F. Buckley a household name.

The show normally had a sort of debate format, and Buckley was a natural entertainer with his WASPy persona, Southern drawl, and prehensile eyebrows. Russell Kirk and James Burnham were vastly greater thinkers than Buckley, as he was the first to admit, but Buckley was far more amusing, which is why he is remembered as the great exponent of American conservatism.

Mencken turned journalism into an art; Buckley turned it into rhetorical battle, and every subsequent television journalist has followed in his footsteps, though without his style, and with shouting increasingly crowding out wit.

Journalists know they can earn far more wealth and celebrity by entertaining their audiences than by informing them. The advent of the internet and "clickbait" has only solidified this trend of media-as-agitprop. The media barons have learned that people don't care about objectivity. They want to be entertained, openly and shamelessly.

The *New York Times*, which had been suffering a long, slow decline, found a second wind in 2016 by developing its own brand of highbrow clickbait. The *Times*'s anti-Trump lobbying was so egregious that its former executive editor, Jill Abramson, publicly condemned her successor's shenanigans. Still, the *Times* forged ahead and became an even more hard-line leftist newspaper, and so far that strategy seems to be working. In 2020, the *Times* hit an all-time high of six million paid subscribers, and digital subscriptions surpassed print subscriptions for the first time in the paper's history.

The media's self-debasement should remind us that an "uninformed" public is far more likely to elect good leaders than one informed by the media. In a republic such as ours, we are not supposed to elect *rulers*, but *lawmakers*. (Even the president is only supposed to execute laws passed by Congress—hence, the *executive* branch.) We ought, then, to choose our lawmakers based on the probity of the laws they would pass. But that is of zero interest to the media, which would rather "inform" readers by inflaming their passions with clickbait.

The whole premise of journalism in the United States is that a cabal of semi-literate alcoholics can arm the public with all the information necessary to make government run efficiently, prudently spend $4 trillion a year, trade with more than 200 foreign countries, and command 1.4 million soldiers stationed in 70 countries. It's all a huge scam. No journalist has any idea what's going on. Do masks help contain the spread of COVID-19? I dunno—and neither do the experts; I can find one to give me any answer I want. Was there voter fraud in the 2020 election? Probably. Enough to flip the result for Mr. Trump? No clue. Did Russians interfere in the 2016 election? They'd be stupid not to. Which side did they help—and did it matter? Haven't the faintest. Nobody does. Sorry, but that's the way it is.

Of course, we hacks can't admit any of that, or else we'd have to find real jobs. The trouble is that we all come to such disparate conclusions. We have to hide the fact that we're all just making things up. So, we insist that only *our* guys are telling the truth, and the *other* guys are lying.

Of course, that means all of those politicians who don't listen to *our* guys are evil. So are the people who vote for them. They can't just be stupid. That would mean our government is too complicated for the average post-pubescent American to operate. It would mean we've outgrown our democracy. No: They have to be wrong on purpose. They have to be evil.

It took a while, but, in the year 2020, we finally knew for certain that half of the country was trying to destroy the other half. If you're a conservative, it's those race-baiting socialists at the DNC and their Antifa goons. If you're a progressive, it's those crypto-fascists at the RNC and their Proud Boy thugs.

As *New York Times* columnist Charles M. Blow wrote in his post–2020 election rundown:

> After all that Donald Trump has done, all the misery he has caused, all the racism he has aroused, all the immigrant families he has destroyed, all the people who have left this life because of the pandemic, still roughly half of the country voted to extend this horror show.... It is so unsettling to consider that many of our fellow countrymen and women are either racists or accommodate racists or acquiesce to racists.

Yes. It's just that simple.

Call me an idealist, but I suspect that most Americans are just astonishingly gullible. We'll embrace any candidate right or left who flatters our belief in our own wisdom and goodness and ability to control the world around us. Take the 2020 election. Donald Trump lost, to a large extent, because he couldn't stop the spread of COVID-19. A sane, healthy *polis* would have realized that's because new viral pandemics take years to fully understand, let alone contain. Yet this would mean we're not in control of the virus. Or any illness, for that matter. Or life. Or death. So, we voted for Joe Biden, who promised more draconian lockdowns to curtail the virus's spread. And we voted for him despite his party's support for left-wing city-burning mobs, open borders for illegal immigrants, and allowing surgically modified men to participate in women's sports—positions that usually aren't considered vote-winners. The bitter reality is that, beneath all our chrome and polyester, we're still the same ignorant serfs who tilled the fields of medieval Europe. We'll follow politicians and journalists more obediently than any French knight ever followed his king or his priest, so long as they pretend that we're still in charge, that we're fully informed.

So, what's the solution? Just tune out. Take it from a professional journalist: never read any journalism, ever. Not even mine. You will be happier, healthier, and better informed.

Walter Hooper tells the story of a conversation he once had with his friend C. S. Lewis about the difference between prettiness and beauty. Hooper proposed Elizabeth Taylor as an example of the latter.

"Who is Elizabeth Taylor?" Lewis asked.

"If you read the newspapers," said Hooper, "you would know who she is."

"Ah!" Lewis cried, "but that is how I keep myself 'unspotted from the world.'" Lewis then suggested that if one "must" read the newspapers, he should make frequent use of "mouthwash": a work of good literature such as *The Lord of the Rings*.

Don't be afraid to be "uninformed."

As T. S. Eliot wrote:

> Where is the wisdom we have lost in knowledge?
> Where is the knowledge we have lost in information?

Susan Sontag, of all people, made an excellent case against mass media:

> Imagine, if you will, someone who read only the *Reader's Digest* between 1950 and 1970, and someone in the same period who read only *The Nation* or the *New Statesman*. Which reader would have been better informed about the realities of communism? The answer, I think, should give us pause. Can it be that our enemies were right?

I don't know who exactly this "enemy" is. I don't know anyone who spent the Cold War urging Americans to ignore the newspapers and settle down with a copy of *Reader's Digest*. But I salute them.

For, truly, men who were ignorant of current events are among the great unsung heroes of modern history. They're the peasants who opposed the Jacobins in France, the Nazis in Germany, and the Communists in Russia. Those wicked movements were all led by a vanguard of intellectuals—men who read all sorts of books and many, many newspapers, and felt their reading entitled them to tell their countrymen what to think and how to act.

It was the peasants, in their simplicity, piety, and common sense, who saw through all the mad theories. A man would have to read a hundred newspapers before he realized that his natural rights were being infringed—or, indeed, that he had any such rights to begin with. He'd have to read a thousand newspapers to understand that the Jews had betrayed Germany in World War I—most likely because he'd fought in the Great War himself, and was inclined to blame his own stupid generals for losing their own stupid war. He'd have to read ten thousand newspapers to realize that Russia needed bureaucrats to collectivize its farms—probably because he'd actually worked on a farm, or at least met a bureaucrat.

That's the wisdom we lost in information. It's wisdom we can only reclaim by cutting ourselves off from the font of all information: the media. So, cancel your subscriptions, close all your browser tabs, and help yourself to a tall glass of mouthwash.

CHAPTER FOURTEEN

Towards a More Blissful Ignorance

To be good and idiotic is not a poor fate but, on the contrary, an experience of primeval innocence, which wonders at all things.
—G. K. Chesterton

At some point in their schooling, all children think to themselves, "This is stupid. I'm never going to use trigonometry when I grow up." And, if we're going to be honest, they're right. As soon as we can read, write, and do long division, we've more or less mastered all of the academic skills necessary for the average person to flourish. This is the dirty little secret that we adults keep to ourselves: school is an utter waste of time.

No responsible parent can help but feel a slight twinge of guilt every morning when he loads his child onto a school bus to spend six hours in a beige-colored room listening to some pedant in a pencil skirt quiz him on *Where the Red Fern Grows*. Dad hated that book. He can't even remember the main character's name. Yet the state will throw him in jail unless he forces his son to go through the same rigamarole. What's the point of it all?

I'm not sure what our forefathers really expected to achieve by making education compulsory, but the only tangible outcome it seems to have is destroying a child's innate love of learning. This is basic child psychology. Force a kid to do something—*anything*—and he automatically doesn't want to do it. He may love history, but make him write a report on the Battle of Gettysburg and he'll groan just as loudly as the dope in the back row. That's what happens when you turn learning into a chore.

Or take literature. Eighty-six percent of Americans can read, and that number is declining. But so what? Most of our countrymen are functionally illiterate anyway. About one quarter of us simply choose not to read, ever. The rest of us spend an average of fifteen minutes a day reading for pleasure. (Those are real statistics, by the way.) And when we do deign to leaf through a book it's likely some rubbishy bestseller that everyone else is reading, such as *Fifty Shades of Grey*—or, for the intellectual, *Harry Potter*. And why? Because our English classes are chock-full of garbage like *A Canticle for Leibowitz* and *The Giver*.

Sure: if students stick it out, they might read *Hamlet* or *The Odyssey*. Still, most people don't care about the great books. Maybe you think they should; I certainly do. Yet surely there's a more efficient way of getting young people to read the classics than threatening to call child services on their parents if they don't.

America's early colleges were meant to produce a natural aristocracy, a class of men whom their fellow citizens would elect to govern our republic, in deference to their wisdom and virtue. Benjamin Franklin founded the University of Pennsylvania to train men with "an inclination...to serve mankind, one's Country, Friends and Family." Donald Trump is the first of our commanders in chief to claim UPenn as his alma mater (do with that as you will). Only twelve U.S. presidents were not college graduates, and that includes just one elected since the turn of the twentieth century (Harry Truman). The system of compulsory schooling continues because it is the principal means by which progressives reproduce themselves.

This idea of co-opting the education system to advance left-wing political goals was forged in the middle of the twentieth century by the selfsame John Dewey. Dewey believed that education ought to "contribute to the values of life" and that the educated man should "add to the decencies and graces of civilization wherever he is." Schools themselves should engage students in "active inquiry and careful deliberation in the significant and vital problems" of the day. Schools were to produce model citizens, and the model citizen was presumed to be the progressive citizen.

This is the explicit goal of America's entire philosophy of education. In 2020, a public school teacher from Philadelphia named Matthew R. Kay expressed concern that conservative parents would have too much control over their children's education unless in-person classes resumed during the COVID-19 pandemic. "We'll never be quite sure who is overhearing the discourse. What does this do for our equity/inclusion work?" Mr. Kay asked. He feared that too much parental involvement would disrupt the schools' "messy work of destabilizing a kid's racism or homophobia or transphobia"—prejudices the child presumably inherited from his right-wing Christian parents.

City Journal reported a similar story in North Carolina's largest school district:

> Parents, according to the teachers, should be considered an impediment to social justice. When one teacher asked, "How do you deal with parent pushback?" the answer was clear: ignore parental concerns and push the ideology of antiracism directly to students. "You can't let parents deter you from the work," the teachers said. "White parents' children are benefiting from the system" of whiteness and are "not learning at home about diversity (LGBTQ, race, etc.)."

Therefore, teachers have an obligation to subvert parental wishes and beliefs. Any "pushback," the teachers explained, is merely because white parents fear "that they are going to lose something" and find it "hard to let go of power [and] privilege."

This isn't an aberration. In fact, the district's official Equity in Action plan encourages teachers to override parents in the pursuit of antiracism. "Equity leaders [should] have the confidence to take risks and make difficult decisions that are rooted in their values," the document reads. "Even in the face of opposition, equity leaders can draw on a heartfelt conviction for what is best for students and families." In other words, the school should displace the family as the ultimate arbiter of political morality.

None of this comes as any surprise to conservatives, who have for decades watched in horror as their children are inculcated with the latest left-wing orthodoxies on race, sex, and "gender." The idea of using tax dollars to pay for women to murder their babies in the womb, or for a little boy to cut off his penis and have it fashioned into a mock vagina, naturally strikes us as cruel and absurd. Ten years or so of public education will help us see past such bigoted views.

If those views somehow survive grade school, they can be purged through years of higher education, which becomes ever more important as our society becomes bureaucratized and more and more jobs require academic—not just work-related—credentials. This credentialing system gives the progressives at the top ever more authority to reward their own yes-men.

J. R. R. Tolkien was a great enemy of credentialism. When the German academy's fetish for doctoral degrees swept across England and America, he refused to accept higher degrees from his beloved

Oxford, which wanted to improve the credentials of its senior faculty. Mind you, Tolkien held three professorial chairs without a Ph.D. He had earned his master's degree, and he took very seriously the proud English tradition which held that a master had mastered his field. He insisted that doctorates were for research specialists, not educators. In 1972, he accepted a doctorate of letters from Oxford, but only because it was a purely ceremonial and honorary degree.

According to one study, in 1940, just over 5 percent of men and less than 3 percent of women had attended a four-year college. By 2019, that number was up to 35 and 36 percent, respectively. And yet—or perhaps not surprisingly—academic standards have fallen so that colleges can make money by graduating as many dullards as possible. In 1892, Harvard required undergraduates to possess "an elementary working knowledge of four languages, two ancient, Latin and Greek, and two modern, French and German," as well as "a knowledge of the history and geography either of ancient Greece and Rome or modern England and America."

In 2005, Ross Douthat wrote about his experience at Harvard:

> Most of my classmates were studious primarily in our avoidance of academic work, and brilliant largely in our maneuverings to achieve a maximal GPA in return for minimal effort. It was easy to see the classroom as just another résumé-padding opportunity, a place to collect the grade (and recommendation) necessary to get to the next station in life. If that grade could be obtained while reading a tenth of the books on the syllabus, so much the better....
>
> Sometimes you didn't have to do even that much....

In short, Harvard offers a degree, not an education.

The most intelligent children I know—the ones who actually enjoy learning, whatever their aptitude—are homeschoolers. If Nazareth offers a model for a humane economy, homeschooling offers a model for a humane education. Curricula and schedules can be tailored to individual students. There's no need for busywork to run down the clock, and no homework. When the kids are done for the day, they can climb trees or go fishing or read a book for pleasure.

That's another thing: recess shouldn't mean standing around on a slab of black asphalt hemmed in by a chain-link fence while teachers stand watch against wandering hordes of perverts. It means walking outside and playing jump rope with your sister, or riding bikes with your brother, or getting together a game of flag football with the other kids in the neighborhood.

This is how you raise a normal, healthy child with normal, healthy interests. Yes, it takes a certain amount of sacrifice and forbearance on the parents' part. But that's true of all parenting—or, at least, of good parenting. And herein lies the problem. While many parents would like to homeschool, it's impossible when both parents are working. And because both parents are working, compulsory education has become a vast, taxpayer-subsidized babysitting service, which fails both as school and as daycare. No parents in their right minds would turn their kids over to the selfless, idealistic members of our corrupt teachers' unions who, during the pandemic, demanded priority in vaccination while still refusing to teach children in classrooms.

That was a light-bulb-going-on moment for many parents: you don't need teachers and schools; you can do it yourself.

I had a similar moment when I was nineteen. I had arrived at the University of Sydney with the intention of becoming an academic. I'd moved to Australia to study with the greatest scholar of T. S. Eliot on the planet, Professor Barry Spurr. My plan was to complete my bachelor's degree with honors, and then it would be on to Oxford for my Ph.D and, from there, to some cozy office in the Ivory Tower.

One day, Barry and I were having lunch after Mass. He asked me if there was any particular course I was looking forward to teaching.

I grimaced. "I don't want to teach."

He looked confused. "Why not?"

"Rambling about poetry to an auditorium full of bored teenagers sounds like hell."

"But then why," he asked, "do you want to be an academic?"

I'd never given the matter any thought. At last, I said, "Because I like books."

"You don't have to be an academic to read books!" Barry cried. That was the moment my life changed forever.

You don't have to be an academic to read books. It was a radical proposition, but the more I turned it over in my mind, the more I suspected he was right.

I'd never been a very good student. I'd gotten a D in AP English my last year of high school because I'd spent the whole year reading Dante and Joyce, ignoring all the coursework. Yet I was also one of the few in my class who liked to read.

The same was true in college. When another professor asked what our class had read over the summer break, I was the only student who didn't say, "Well, uhhh, just some articles I saw on Facebook and, like, yeah." Yet I had to transfer out of half my classes to avoid failing out. (Two weeks into a seminar on Jane Austen, I realized that I hated her novels and refused to read anything she'd written.) Until Barry's intervention, it never once occurred to me that I might get a real job and read in my spare time.

The majority of those who read today read under compulsion. They are students. In other words, we do most of our reading under the direction of teachers. And I suspect that authors have begun (perhaps unconsciously) pandering to schoolteachers. They don't seek to write *great* novels, but teachable ones.

What's the difference? Well, there are any number of writers that critics would universally describe as "great," and yet who seldom make it into high school or college curricula. *Brideshead Revisited* by Evelyn Waugh is one example. It's not taught because there's very little to teach. The prose is clear and humorous. The social themes (class and whatnot) are fairly straightforward. It's a deeply religious novel, but not an especially profound one. A lot of people are having sex with people they oughtn't to be; they stop, and are better for it. The end.

Contrast this with something like *A Portrait of the Artist as a Young Man* by James Joyce. It's horribly written and manifestly fails as a work of art. But it's eminently teachable. There's lots for school-teachers to "contextualize." They can discuss the stream-of-consciousness style and its impact on high modernism. They can talk about its themes of exile, and how it relates to the Irish republican movement. They can talk about Joyce's rejection of "Catholic guilt." They can talk about his embrace of the cult of the artist, which sees the poet as a kind of priest, transubstantiating the raw material of everyday life into something sublime and edifying, and its roots in the Aestheticism of Oscar Wilde—who, paradoxically, rejected Aestheticism at the end of his life and became a Catholic.

Do you see? A novel is teachable when it gives the teacher a lot to talk about besides the novel. That's the ideal. Because, with really *good* literature, the author says everything there is to say. That's why he's the author, and you're not. You can't teach a good novel; you just read it.

The successful novels of our own age are those that include lots of "context." That's why Zadie Smith's *On Beauty* is included in so many high school reading lists. With all due respect to Ms. Smith, it's an incredibly pretentious book. The ethno-political dynamic of Harvard University isn't something that interests—or should interest—ordinary teenagers. Yet, for the average American high school *teacher*, a novel about race in an Ivy League school is perfect for inculcating kids with current race obsessions.

The education most of us get in school is worthless. That's all right. These days, the only educated man is the autodidact, and the reactionary almost invariably has a well-stocked library. See the appendices for how to stock yours.

CHAPTER FIFTEEN

Technoholics Anonymous

*"And now we know what it feels like for the Jinn," said
Edmund with a chuckle. "Golly! It's a bit uncomfortable
to know that we can be whistled for like that. It's worse
than what Father says about living at the mercy of the
telephone."*
—C. S. Lewis

I'm told that I have an irrational fear of flying. Of course, that's
exactly wrong. I have a perfectly rational fear of flying, which
every biped ought to share. Nothing appeals to me about the
prospect of hurtling through the ether, six miles from the ground, at
six hundred miles per hour, in a giant cigar tube. Surely it's everyone
else who has an insane faith in the power of airplanes.

Now, before you say anything, I know that man is an inventive
animal. I know that his bold confidence in that genius for invention
is part of his glory. And I suppose that an aeronautical engineer—
someone who truly understands the mechanics and physics of air
travel—might find some masochistic pleasure in launching himself
thirty thousand feet into the air and seeing if he can get back to earth
again without dying in a fiery holocaust.

Some people also enjoy standing in front of a charging bull and seeing if they can leap away in time to avoid being gored. Yet, if I told you I had no special desire to become a matador, you probably wouldn't accuse me of suffering from a phobia.

The idea that we groundlings are psychologically defective is absurd. Ninety-nine percent of those who do fly haven't the faintest idea how airplanes work. Nor are they especially brave. They rattle off statistics about how you're more likely to die in a car crash, as if that were some ringing endorsement. Loggers technically suffer a higher mortality rate than American soldiers, and yet few of us are lining up to vacation in Kabul.

In the end, it has nothing to do with engineering. Those statistics are only lies we tell ourselves to avoid the larger truth, which is that we have an unthinking, cultish faith in the voodoo spirit called "science." For the overwhelming majority of us, a Boeing 747 may as well be a winged horse or a flying carpet. But Perseus's faith in the gods of Olympus, or Aladdin's in the magic of his djinn, pales in comparison to our belief in science. And, so, we board that plane without a moment's hesitation. We gaze down at the clouds without so much as a sense of wonder, as if we were looking at a foam-flecked riverbank.

That, I think, is the real trouble with our modern Icarus. It's not the flying itself. It's the fact that flying became so quickly just another way of getting around. Most of us are more likely, in the course of a year, to fly halfway across the country than we are to ride a bicycle to the corner store. This truly remarkable thing, flight—a thing that, for us bipeds, ought to be shrouded in fear and mystery and delight—is hardly more impressive than sharpening a pencil.

Surely, this is the definition of hubris. At least the old Icarus marveled at the world beneath his wings before they melted in the sun and sent him tumbling into the sea.

To the objective observer, there can be little doubt that our inventiveness has gotten the better of us. We're utterly dependent on these technologies. We're ruled by our own machines. And much technology does far more harm than good. Yet we can't imagine life without it, because we refuse to try.

Let's go on with the example of airplanes. I agree with Chesterton that travel narrows the mind. I will go further and say that tourism makes the world seem incredibly cramped. Easy travel and commerce were supposed to lead to a great exchange of cultures and ideas. We were all meant to have universal access to the best that each glorious people had to offer. But, in fact, what have we in the West derived from these cultures? We took the Native American peace pipe and reduced it to menthol cigarettes. We took Columbian coffee beans and crammed them into a Keurig cup. We took the Arabian Peninsula and refined it into gasoline.

In retrospect, I wonder how it could have been otherwise. We tell ourselves that we're worldly because we have the world at our fingertips. But beneath all our Korean plastics and Malaysian polyester, we're still delightfully provincial. We have no great interest in Confucian philosophy, though we help ourselves to Chinese wage slaves. We're very fond of pizza, though not so much of Dante or Petrarch.

And that's all right. (The provinciality, I mean. Not the wage slaves.) In more provincial ages, the sort of men who really enjoyed diving into foreign cultures tended to be rather unbalanced—T. E. Lawrence, for instance. They usually weren't embracing a new people so much as rejecting their own. But they understood one obvious truth that we somehow can't grasp. "Culture" isn't something one can sample at a restaurant after a movie. It can't be "appreciated" in a week's vacation. Culture is an entire way of life. It has to be lived to be understood.

Let me give an example. As a younger man, I studied Islam with a great Sufi master. I loved Sufi poetry, and still do. I love their ubiquitous metaphor, that being in the presence of the Divine is like getting drunk on wine. But here's the thing: the Sufis, like all Muslims, don't drink. That's why, when they describe their mystical intoxication, it sounds so beautiful and wholesome—nothing at all like Saint Patrick's Day in South Boston. They're like eunuchs writing love songs: their desire is pure because it will never be consummated, and they know it. We who do drink wine, and drink it in abundance, can never truly understand what they mean. We might admire the Sufis, as outsiders, but we can no more drop in and out of Rumi than we can drop in and out of love.

This is the first thing we must understand about multiculturalism. It doesn't allow us to immerse ourselves in many different cultures at once. It merely strips out the really challenging or alien parts. It whittles down some ancient and venerable society into little bite-sized pieces. It's cultural consumerism. And it's usually restricted to the most extrinsic parts: clothes, food, and maybe the odd "traditional proverb." But the truly rich variety of human life—the ethics and mores, the religion and philosophy, the things that make sense of life and give it meaning—are pulled out and discarded like the spine of a fish. Of course, the spine might not suit our purposes. But it's rather important to the fish.

The second is like unto it: a man can't be cultured and "multicultural" at the same time. How can I expect to appreciate a Shinto temple if I won't even pray in a Catholic church? How could I understand the ritual of seppuku when I pooh-pooh the Christian code of chivalry? A Westerner can't appreciate the traditions of Japan when he's rejected his own homegrown traditions. That's like saying you never had any children yourself because you feel a paternal affection for all children, everywhere in the world. It's absurd: you can't even begin to know what paternal affection feels like unless you are yourself a pater. You're going to wind up with some fuzzy, Disneyfied idea that being a dad is all about playing catch and giving sage advice, just as some people (including a heartbreaking number of Japanese) think the Far East is all about bowing at the waist and watching anime.

There's nothing quite so surreal as watching an American progressive argue that we should embrace polygamy for the sake of accommodating Muslim immigrants. Progressives genuinely don't seem to realize that, were the situations reversed, Muslims would then have to embrace monogamy for the sake of accommodating Western immigrants. If every people on earth made it a priority to "accommodate" the other, then there would be no culture left anywhere.

And, in fact, that's exactly what's playing out before our eyes. Everywhere in the developed world, from Paris to Peking, people shop for clothes at the same Zara outlet, eat the same McDonald's hamburgers, watch the same Hollywood films, and stare blankly into the same iPhones, punching out the same incoherent string of emojis and gifs and LOLs, SMHs, and TTYLs.

Many conservatives believe that progressives' obsession with "inclusivity" arises from a hatred for their own Western, predominantly white, predominantly Christian culture. I'm not so sure. It seems more likely that they're so enamored of their own multiculturalism that they've entirely forgotten what it means to inhabit a culture of their own. They're so caught up in the cheap trinkets we've borrowed from other peoples that they've forgotten how to relate to their own people. They think the West is just a vast museum of international kitsch. That's all they've ever known.

Case in point: A few years ago, there was a great panic on the left over "cultural appropriation." It was deemed intolerably offensive for white men to wear their hair in dreadlocks or for white women to wear kimonos. Naturally, in every single instance, there was no intention to offend. The appropriators were paying homage to the culture from which they were appropriating. They recognized something beautiful and meaningful in that culture—something, perhaps, they couldn't find in their own culture, which has all but vanished from public view to be replaced by the anti-culture of multiculturalism and consumer capitalism.

For conservatives, this was just another opportunity to flap their arms and complain about "political correctness gone mad," the hypocrisy of progressives, who, if they were serious, should take offense at Japanese women wearing jeans, or mixed-race men whose dreadlocks didn't represent the exact proportion of their African blood. All good fun, but, as usual, conservatives squandered an opportunity to make a really meaningful point about globalism. For the anti-appropriationists were inspired by a perfectly wholesome, even reactionary instinct. It was a desire to treat venerable cultures and customs with reverence, to save them from becoming yet another lousy dish in our all-you-can-eat multicultural buffet. If we no longer tap into our own traditions, we may as well show some respect for theirs.

Besides, only the most atomized and deracinated white people would ever want to wear a kimono or put their hair in dreads, customs which have no meaning or value to them beyond a sense of the exotic.

And that, perhaps, is the whole point. That's where the movement against cultural appropriation fell apart. We can't reverence other cultures because we're not allowed to revere our own. We can't conceive of what it's like to attach such profound meaning to a hairstyle or a garment. We can't empathize with most non-Western peoples because we have no living traditions ourselves.

What conservatives should have done was tell their progressive friends to go hug a Confederate soldier statue—as if they (I mean the conservatives) would have the guts to do that—or a Union soldier statue or a statue of Columbus or Washington or Lincoln or Jefferson or Franklin or any of the other targets of leftist iconoclasm, or to celebrate Thanksgiving without qualms, or the Fourth of July without irony, or to actually, you know, stand and sing the national anthem, hand or hat over heart, at a baseball game. That's the irony (and the tragedy) of multiculturalism—or tolerance, or diversity, or whatever you like to call it. Cultures are born of people who share a common way of life, live in the same environment, raise the same crops, rear the same animals, speak the same language, have the same customs, sing the same songs, share the same heroes, and worship the same gods. Anyone who tries to be Anglo on Monday, Arabian on Tuesday, Jamaican on Wednesday, and Japanese on Thursday will be nothing—nobody—on Friday. He'll be an immigrant from Nowhere in the land of Wherever. He'll forever be a tourist, never a countryman. So, I say again: travel narrows the mind.

But our woes began even before the advent of air travel. They go back at least to the automobile—or, as Russell Kirk called them, mechanical Jacobins.

After all, tradition doesn't begin with the nation. It begins with the family. Then it grows into the community, which is a kind of federation of families. And cars have done more to destroy communities than the French Revolution could have dreamed. They've been a more radicalizing influence than 100,000 Robespierres.

Before the age of mass transit, if a man was a farmer, he seldom strayed more than a few acres from his front door. If he was a craftsman, his workshop was usually just the ground floor of his house. Except for ambassadors and soldiers, the idea of "traveling for work" was unheard of. The nearest that most folks came to a business trip was a cobbler walking down Main Street to see if the postman needed new shoes.

One of the few upsides to the coronavirus pandemic is that we're finally beginning to do away with this unnatural idea of commuting.

Surely, nothing has proven more destructive to the family than forcing most fathers (and, now, most mothers) out of the house for at least nine hours a day.

We say that a man is supposed to be the head of his household. If so, he's been an absentee for centuries. In the old days, if a dad needed to make some weighty decision, or settle a dispute, or dispense some paternal wisdom, or discipline a wayward youngling, he had only to come in from the field for half an hour. If his wife or his children wanted to spend some time with him, they could come downstairs and shoot the breeze while helping to sweep the floor or stock the shelves. The family ate breakfast, lunch, and dinner together, because a man's only breakroom was his kitchen. Dads were on call twenty-four hours a day, seven days a week. And, somehow, we got by.

Today, fatherhood is something a man can only do in his spare time—after work, when he's exhausted and grumpy, or on the weekend, when he's supposed to be enjoying a little rest. And with the influx of women into the workforce, it's a wonder that either mom or dad has the energy to be a parent, which is why the demand for nannies has never been higher.

Conservatives complain endlessly about the decline of the traditional family. They complain that men and women put off marriage and child-rearing to focus on their careers. And they're right to complain. Yet how many of them realize that, since the rise of Commuterland, we've trained men to put work before family? We've always told them to put their employers first and their children second, if anywhere. Force a man to spend most of his waking hours at work, and it's only natural that fatherhood should become more like a hobby: something we do in our downtime, like softball or poker.

Naturally, fathers have to work. We are providers; that's an integral part of our role. But *integral* is the key word here. In the good old days, all aspects of life were integrated. A man's home was his farm or workshop, and vice versa. His aunts and uncles and cousins and siblings were his customers. His children were his apprentices and helpers.

Today, the demands of consumer capitalism force us to rigidly segregate our private and public selves. It's a kind of economically induced schizophrenia. And then, adding insult to injury, we talk about the need to keep "a healthy work-life balance"! Make sure that your split personalities are playing nice, everyone.

I say don't balance work and life. Abolish that false and inhuman dichotomy. Work is integral to life, and life is integral to work.

The great new integrator of our lives, however, is not the family business but the most dangerous and lamentable invention in history: the screen.

Not a day goes by without some Big Brain's warning about the dangers of artificial reality. It's hard not to laugh. According to the latest Nielsen statistics, American adults spend eleven hours a day "consuming media"—that is, staring at screens (smartphones, television, computers, laptops, tablets, et al.). Assuming they sleep for eight hours a night, that leaves five hours of consciousness unmediated by the ubiquitous screen.

Let's not kid ourselves. We're already living in a virtual reality. Who can deny it? And no man has a right to speak of "freedom" who is willingly enslaved to his devices. No man has the right to speak of "truth" who allows his entire experience of the world to be mediated by Apple or Microsoft, Twitter or Facebook, Fox News or CNN.

I don't have a cell phone or a television. I don't have a social media or Netflix or Amazon Prime account. I get my news from a local newspaper, to which I subscribe mostly for the crosswords. I'm writing these words with a pencil on a yellow legal pad. My digital life is minimal, and entirely work-related. Whenever we can break away from screens, we should.

The mother of all screens is the television. By today's standards, TV is a relatively minor monster. But it possesses the two qualities that make all screen-based life inferior. These qualities, as the great John Senior put it, are *radical passivity* and *distortion of reality*.

The screen subverts and ultimately sublimates our intellect, our imagination. What we see effectively bypasses our rational mind and enters directly into the subconscious, which is why I can still recite every line from the first five seasons of *The Simpsons* from memory, but have trouble remembering my own birthday. With television, we don't think, we merely absorb.

This makes television the perfect vehicle for entertainment. It requires no effort on our part. It's also why conservatives have rightly feared its influence over children, even as, typically, they've acquiesced to it.

It's astonishing that more people haven't drawn the parallel between screens and Plato's cave. Then again, maybe it isn't. The whole point is that most men will choose the dumb familiarity of the cave over the harsh, bracing sunlight of reality. If it were obvious, it wouldn't be worth commenting on. But apparently it isn't, and so it is.

Still, we're only splashing around in the shallows. In the blink of an eye, computers and smartphones have superseded television as the ordinary American's screen of choice. Only the latter can be carried on our person, ensuring that we have an uninterrupted stream of stimuli available 'round the clock.

Surely I don't need to go through all the statistics that prove these technologies are an unmitigated evil. I don't need to tell you that using a smartphone for any period of time is scientifically proven to stunt your attention span and make it more difficult to sleep at night. I don't need to remind you that the flashing lights given off by these little screens massively contribute to anxiety disorders. You already know that social media is designed after the slot machine, creating dopamine feedback loops that will leave you jonesing for likes and "favs" and retweets. Everybody's heard that Instagram and Snapchat are the leading cause of body insecurity, depression, and suicide among young Americans. Most likely, you're even aware that social media debates cause the same psychochemical response as road rage. You literally get high off being mean to strangers on the internet. And you probably know that, like road rage, it's powerfully addictive. You've probably even heard of the "online disinhibition effect": how we all find it much easier being cruel to other human beings when we don't have to look them in the face—again, like road rage.

All of this is common knowledge. And, in rare moments of clarity, there's no doubt in your mind that these devices make your life immeasurably worse. You know that you and everyone you interact with would be much happier if you deleted all of your apps and accounts and chucked your iPhone into a river. In fact, at some point today, you probably made a to-do list of all the things you hope to accomplish in the next day or week or year—appliances you want to fix, relatives you want to call, books you want to read, skills you want to learn, trips you want to take, real-life experiences you want to have—most of which you know you'll never get around to, because it would mean cutting into your screen time. And, despite your best intentions, you know that's one sacrifice you're not willing to make.

I'm not trying to make you feel ashamed, dear reader. Quite the contrary. I'm trying to help you. I want you to recognize that you're in the throes of a nasty addiction. Because you must realize that, if digital technology were a substance you smoked or drank, you would demand that the government regulate it heavily, if not ban it outright. At the very least, you would plead with your younger and purer self not to touch the stuff in the first place.

Yes, we are in the midst of a pandemic far more dangerous than the opioid or COVID-19. This disease will affect ninety-nine out of every one hundred Americans. It robs us of our capacity for rational thought and independent judgment. It makes us peevish and narrow-minded. And, as with all addictions, we laugh cruelly at anyone who urges us to kick the habit.

That shiny black rectangle in your pocket promises endless entertainment, and except for God and deep space, it's the nearest we'll ever come to infinity: it's always waiting at our fingertips. How could we *not* lose ourselves? How could we not go mad?

We also find that, like space (though unlike God), it's also banal. But that's part of the reason we like it so much. Unlike friendship, or literature, or prayer, it's not difficult. It asks nothing of us. It's perfectly mindless, and we may take that literally. Why not spend our lives in that vast sea of banality, where there's always a new sensation and laziness is actually a virtue?

We used to talk about the "infinite scroll," but now many call it the "doom scroll," which hints at that feeling of resignation in modern man, who seems to realize that he's almost fated to spend (at least!) eleven hours a day gazing into that blue-lit abyss for the rest of his life.

If there is an afterlife, our technocholic will surely regret the way he spent this one. Again, we have Screwtape telling his protégé that a man arrives in hell saying, "I now see that I spent most my life in doing neither what I ought nor what I liked." Yes, your smartphone is hell.

The good news is that conservatives are awakening to the need to pull our countrymen from the abyss. Senator Josh Hawley has been advancing legislation that would ban autoplay videos and the "doom scroll." I wish him well. But Big Tech will always find new and more ingenious ways to make its drug more addictive. It's how Big Tech makes money.[1] Even the most well-meaning government can only ever play catch-up. By the time we've put out one fire, the tech gurus will have lit ten more.

Anyway, the solution can't be political, because the problem isn't political. The problem, ultimately, is the deadly sin of sloth. And so the only real solution is an individual act of *will*. So, the answer is clear: smash your smartphone—not only for your sake, but for the sake of all mankind. For surely you've noticed that digital technology has poisoned the well of politics in the developed world?

Twitter is what's technically known as a "microblogging" platform. You can't help but chuckle at the name. It's as though blogging itself were such a great success that we had to make the whole process quicker and easier so more folks could do it. There weren't enough people who spent their leisure hours bludgeoning each other with their opinions on the internet, so we had to seize the means of production and distribute them equally among the masses.

How could that *not* damage the tone of our discourse? Politics is unpleasant by its nature. It was long considered inappropriate for dinner table chitchat, because nobody really cares what anyone else thinks. If we happen to agree, it's all well and good. But, if we don't, very few of us can actually agree to disagree like gentlemen. Usually, you wind up shouting at one another until one of you hurls a gravy boat at the other, and your wife tearfully begs you to take her home before someone gets maimed.

Yet thanks to the internet (particularly social media), you can log on and pick a fight with someone you don't know and don't care about any time of the day or night. And you can fight about anything: a movie neither of you has seen, a policy issue neither of you has studied, or a bill neither of you has read. There are no consequences whatsoever.

Well, no immediate consequences.

There's nothing wrong with arguing with strangers about politics per se. But, in the good old days, a conservative had to go find a seedy bar near the docks if he wanted to have a go at a socialist. Now, if you've ever actually tried this out (as I have), you'll know that there's a natural "cap" to how heated the rhetoric can become. You won't say anything that will get you dragged into the parking lot and socked in the mouth, and you'll come to the realistic conclusion that you're unlikely to change anyone's mind by arguing.

The great danger of social media is that it subverts all these natural checks on our behaviors. Chances are "keyboard warriors" would be much more polite and understanding if they actually had to look the other guy in the eye (or the fist.)

When I tell my conservative friends they should quit Twitter because it is inherently shallow, crass, and cruel, they always make the same excuse: "Why should we cede this whole platform to the Left? Why should we hand them such a massive advantage over us?" Well, first, because the platform itself is evil. Second, because progressives will always have the advantage on social media. It's their home field. These are their platforms. They're owned and operated by, and for, progressives.

It used to be that when lefties wanted to disseminate some new error they had to push it through Congress. That meant beginning a campaign in the newspapers—and, before that, fighting any number of lawsuits against obscenity laws or blasphemy laws or what have you. This would take years, decades, sometimes centuries. Today, all they have to do is start a new hashtag. On a good day, the Left can push through two or three brand-new errors without cramping their thumbs.

So, conservatives are scrambling to develop and consolidate behind new social media platforms of their own. For a while it was Gab, until that site was overwhelmed by racist frogs. At the moment, it's Parler, Signal, and something called MeWe.

But consider this. If our whole justification for staying on social media is to win over left-wing readers, how does forming own little ghetto of the internet advance that cause? All it does is lower our own level of discourse to that of the stupid, nasty progressives on Twitter, only perhaps less vulgar and more sarcastic. I hope nobody is under the illusion that progressives and moderates are going to flock to conservative sites. I can assure you, they're not desperate to hear conservatives' perspectives on events of the day. That's why Big Tech initially moved against Parler. The Left wants to shut you up, not listen to you.

And after it shuts you up, it's going to flood you with its own politics, gossip, memes, selfies, and ads. Oh, so many ads. I read a study once that said the average American encounters about ten thousand ads every day. Corporations pay top dollar so that, 3.7 million times a year, that shiny black rectangle in your pocket will try to sell you face scrub, or yoga pants, or robots that will vacuum your floor.

A healthy society cannot exist under these circumstances. "Good mental health" is totally out of the question. All this advertising and endless chatter will drive you insane, if only in a small way. What does it mean to be insane, except to be divorced from reality?

The reactionary agrees with Jesus Christ that we ought to love our neighbor as ourselves. But we also agree with Robert Frost that good fences make good neighbors. We believe it's easier to love our fellow man when we can keep a healthy distance for the most part.

That's why I love the Carthusians. Members of this ancient order live in community but only speak during communal prayer. They work, study, and eat in silence. The modern world would call this anti-social, and maybe even elitist. But their goal isn't to retreat from mankind or stand in judgment on it. On the contrary. As the Anglican bishop Gordon Mursell wrote in a lovely little book on the Carthusians, their spirituality

> included an approach to human love as profound and coherent as anything found in Provence or Champagne, or recovered from classical antiquity. Love, for the Carthusians, involved an unequivocal detachment from the world, but only as a means to an end; for they saw that detachment as setting them free to love both man and God as each should be loved. The Carthusian life, in the eyes of its founders, involved not a rejection of human love, but its transfiguration.

In other words, the less you talk to other people, the easier it is to love them. Well, that seems about right to me.

Now, I must sound *really* anti-social. But listen: if you've ever spent any amount of time in (say) a Maine fishing village, you'll have noticed two things. First, people don't talk to one another. If you're "from away," they don't even make eye contact. Second, they'd do anything for anyone. "I need help getting my boat in the water." Okay, done. "I need a kidney." Sure, fine. I'll put my supper in the oven and meet you at the hospital.

This used to be the way everyone was, everywhere. Because they loved their neighbors. They weren't "interconnected" by technology; they were a real community. And that's a very different thing. Communities thrive or die only insofar as they work together. Community is about coming together. It's also about leaving one another alone.

Of course, purging the world of planes and cars and computers may prove a bit tricky. But let's put last things first. If you want to break the interconnection of technology and build a real community, here's what you must do.

First, delete every social media account you have. Facebook, Twitter, Instagram, Pinterest, LinkedIn—everything. Don't say good-bye to your "friends." Don't delay for a moment. Delete your accounts. All of them.

Second, get a hammer out of your toolbox. Put your phone on the ground. (No tiled floors, please.) Now, apply the head of the hammer swiftly and repeatedly to your phone until it's dead.

Third, get a flip phone or a landline if need be. If you opt for the dumbphone, never carry it in your pocket. Leave it in a drawer or in your car. Only surgeons and priests should be "on call." Don't surrender an ounce of your privacy, your independence, your peace of mind, to a mere device. If you want to have a conversation, meet for a beer and a smoke.

And, if people want to get in touch with you, let them send you an email. This may seem counterintuitive, from a Luddite's perspective. Certainly an ink-and-paper letter, sent with a stamp by snail mail, would be preferable. But we must learn to walk before we run, and at least with email you can appoint fifteen minutes of your day to checking your inbox and replying to correspondence. You go to *it*; it doesn't barge in on *you*. It doesn't ping or buzz or light up. It waits patiently in the ether until you condescend to address it. Email is the kind of software a man can do business with.

This, dear reader, is the first and most necessary step towards becoming a reactionary. If a chap isn't willing to make this one small sacrifice for the sake of his own happiness, his own freedom, then he isn't worthy of the name. All the Twitter trolls with Thomas Aquinas as their profile pictures and Maistre quotes in their bios are worthless to us. The reactionary is one who lives in open revolt against modernity, against "progress"—beginning, as King Ludd did, by torching those dark satanic mills.

Sic semper tyrannis.

CHAPTER SIXTEEN

The Patient Arts

*Just as the fear of God is the beginning of wisdom, silence
is the beginning of the fear of God.*
— Søren Kierkegaard

N ow that we've all beaten our smartphones to death in a righteous fury, we'll have upwards of eleven free hours a day.
That might sound terrific, but it isn't—at least, not at first.

The life of a Luddite is far richer in the long run. As time goes on,
you'll find your attention span lengthening. You'll be able to read for
an hour (or more!) at a time. Your eyes will be able to pick up more
detail; you'll suddenly notice birds sitting on trees and flowers poking
through the snow. You'll be able to engage other people more easily;
your conversations will be longer and more fluid. You'll fall asleep
more quickly at night, and sleep more deeply. You'll wake up refreshed
and with more energy. You'll enjoy life more, because whenever you
do something meaningful—such as read or talk or lie down in bed—
you won't be itching to check your Facebook or browse listicles on
"forty-seven cartoons every nineties kid will remember."

But, in the short term, the effects of technology withdrawal can
be hell. Your attention span will have been so stunted by Netflix and

YouTube that having to amuse yourself with *anything* besides those flashing lights piped directly into your eyeholes will be agony. Like any junkie weaning himself off a drug, it will take time for your brain to go back to normal.

You'll have to find something to do with all of that hideous, oppressive free time. This is the perfect time to rediscover what I call the Patient Arts.

The Patient Arts are just what they sound like. They're true, good, and beautiful things that only people with real powers of concentration can enjoy (that is, basically everyone who was born before the advent of television). They endow each moment with purpose and satisfaction. They teach one to find enjoyment in small, quiet details. They are, at best, a kind of meditation or prayer, useful, purposeful. They refresh mind, soul, and body.

The most obvious example is reading. Literature may be the most perfect art; at least, it's the most populist. It's the only true art that's accessible to the masses. Great music should be heard live, with real instruments. Great paintings should be seen in person: real paint on real canvas. But a great story, or a great poem, can be appreciated anywhere that ink meets paper. One can read Keats in a stately leather-bound volume, or in a dainty pocket-sized collection with gilt-edged paper, or in a trade paperback. It's all the same. Actually, I prefer trade paperbacks. They're less distracting. One can fold the pages over and hold them in one hand while rocking the baby's crib or what have you.

With trade paperbacks, one can also write in the margins without feeling any guilt. This is probably a point of some contention among my fellow reactionaries. I know some who can't bear the thought of writing in books; I know others who can't concentrate on what they're reading *without* writing in the book. One can't help but recall Saint Augustine's astonishment at discovering that his mentor Saint

Ambrose could read silently. "His eyes scanned the page and his heart sought out the meaning," Augustine remarked, "but his voice was silent and his tongue was still." Apparently, being able to read without even moving one's lips was an achievement in the late Roman Empire.

But, with the exception of the Bible, I think it's good to write in books when one can. To find a really good book is like falling in love. As two lovers get to know each other, they each leave their mark on the other's soul. For better or for worse, they change each other irrevocably. A good book will certainly change you, and I don't see why you shouldn't change it.

I say "for better or for worse" because I sometimes find old copies of books I loved as a teenager, and not only do I now hate the books, but I hate my own scribbles even more. Our first books, like our first loves, make some of the deepest impressions; they also make some of the worst.

When you're not reading a good book, try writing a good letter. You might only write one a day; it might narrow your circle of "friends," but the interactions will be much more meaningful than selfies or 280-character snippets.

When you sit down to write a letter, you'll notice that it changes the way you think. You become a little more courteous, a little more dignified. Your language is more precise, because your writing hand (unlike your texting thumbs) can't move as quickly as your brain. And because it takes more effort to print than to type, you also quickly learn the "economy of language": saying what you need to say as briefly and as elegantly as possible.

Best of all, though, is the joy you bring to someone when he opens his mailbox and finds a real-life envelope containing a real-life letter. If you've ever received one yourself (it's sad to think how many men and women my age probably haven't), you'll know exactly what I mean. The fact that someone you love loves you enough to put all that effort into writing you a letter! Clearly, they think you're a cut above the rest, who only get those mass e-blasts on social media and maybe the occasional text.

Keep a journal. It's fun to look back after years and months and see what was on your mind. But it also has a way of putting things into perspective. When you have this special place reserved for introspection, petty slights or political rows have a tendency to melt from one's mind. You discover depths of yourself you might never have known about before. And then it becomes a new habit. You're like a child in a pool: once you can dive off the diving board, you don't want to waste all your time splashing around in the shallows.

Write poetry. Make sure it has rhyme and meter and all that. Frost said that free verse—poetry that lacks rhyme, meter, and everything else that makes it real poetry—is like playing tennis without a net. He's right. Discipline in writing disciplines your thoughts; when you refine your language, you refine your sentiments. Half the fun of writing a poem is the challenge of finding the perfect word to express your thought; the other half is finding another word that rhymes with the first one. Wordsworth called poetry "emotion recollected in tranquility," which is as good a definition as any, and we should cultivate that sense of tranquility.

Don't worry about sending your poems to magazines. If they're bad, they probably won't get published; if they're good, they don't stand a chance. Besides, the reactionary is a great proponent of amateurism: doing things not for money or fame, but for the fun of it.

If you're a man, the dashing, hard-drinking, womanizing Cavalier poets who fought for King Charles I in the English Civil War should be your model. Their poems are about love and war, God and philosophy, wooing women and drinking with men, and never, never whining about the state of the world.[1]

The best-known verse of the Cavalier school is "To His Coy Mistress" by Andrew Marvell. It begins, "Had we but world enough and time,/This coyness, lady, were no crime."

Her coyness, in fact, would be charming: "I would/ Love you ten years before the flood,/And you should, if you please, refuse/Till the conversion of the Jews."

But they have neither time nor world enough: "at my back I always hear/ Time's winged chariot hurrying near." So, she should forget her modesty. If not, they'll soon both be dead, and

> worms shall try
> That long-preserved virginity,
> And your quaint honour turn to dust,
> And into ashes all my lust . . .

I can't say I approve of the message, but it's manly stuff, and I'm sure his drinking buddies at the tavern got a kick out of it.

Here's another rule of thumb: when in doubt, an amateur should make his poem funny. If you're trying to write a truly *great* poem, of course, do as you must. And if you find you have some truly noble sentiment you want to put down in verse, by all means. But if you just feel like playing around with a rhyme, and you want to share it with your friends, go for a laugh.

Some friends and I trade satiric poems back and forth. Usually, we just riff off a better-known poem. Here's a favorite of mine by W. B. Yeats:

> "A Drinking Song"
> By W. B. Yeats
>> Wine comes in at the mouth
>> And love comes in at the eye;

That's all we shall know for truth
Before we grow old and die.
I lift the glass to my mouth,
I look at you, and I sigh.

And here's my homage:

"A Hangover Song"
By M. W. Davis
Whisky comes in at the mouth
And money just falls from the sky;
That's all we can handle for truth
Before we spill over and cry.
I lift one more glass to my mouth,
And feel like I'm going to die.

It's not exactly Swift, but we got a kick out of it.

What else?

Learn an instrument. Some conservatives seem to be prejudiced against simple instruments, such as guitars and pennywhistles. It's most common among those who think conservatism is a kind of snobbish Anglophilia (which, for all I know, it is). But good, solid, peasantish people have been playing simple string and wind instruments from time immemorial. They didn't have court musicians to give private concerts of Mozart symphonies, so they made the music themselves.

A simple, peasantish soul can appreciate both high and low culture in their place. The low meets him where he is, and the high exalts him. But he always comes back down to earth. Besides, the pleasure of music isn't only in the hearing. It can also be in the playing and the singing—not to mention the toasting, the dancing, and the romancing. Girls always sing a little better when they're trying to impress a special someone, and boys always sing a little worse. That's part of the fun.

But, yes, learn to accompany the singing on the guitar, the flute, even the fiddle. Learn the piano, and lead your friends and family in carols at Christmas. Listening to music is all right, but nothing makes a party better than everyone's belting out some catchy old tune.

In college, my fellow reactionaries and I would get drunk on scotch, sing the Kaiserhymne, and weep manly tears. Real men *do* cry, but not for themselves. They cry for dead heroes and lost causes. They cry for something greater than themselves.

And they smoke.[2] Now, this is a matter of some debate among reactionaries. Most will say that reactionaries categorically reject cigarettes. I myself wouldn't be so absolute. They work in a pinch. Besides, T. S. Eliot killed himself smoking "brutal black French cigarettes," so they can't be all bad.

I feel a much greater prejudice against cigars. I understand the conquistadors smoked them, and if there are any conquistadors hanging around, they have my blessing. But the iconic cigar-smokers of our time are the Cuban Communist Fidel Castro and the British liberal Winston Churchill, both disreputable. Today, cigars are favored mostly by middle-aged, middle-class men who want to play at being middle-aged, upper-middle-class men, and also by ambitious young hacks making their way up the bottom three rungs of the Republican establishment's power ladder. Cigars are impossible to finish and impossible to inhale. The smell clings to one's clothes for weeks and weeks, and somehow manages to be even more offensive than cigarette smoke. I can't see the appeal. But I believe this is one area where we may agree to disagree.

There's no question, however, that the pipe is the reactionary's go-to means of consuming tobacco smoke. This is true for any number of reasons—besides the obvious facts that it tastes the best, smells the best, and costs the least.

We say, "Man is a creature of habit." It would be a little more accurate to say that he's a creature of ritual. Steve might have a habit of drinking too much at parties and having to sleep on the couch, but that tells us something about Steve. It doesn't tell us anything about man. Habits tell us about individuals; rituals tell us about our humanity.

The most common expression of ritual is religious liturgy, and it's no surprise that every traditional culture in the world has developed some careful rites that its members perform with great solemnity to honor their gods. It might be the circle dance of the Native Americans, or the whirling of the Sufi dervishes, or the Holy Sacrifice of the Mass in the Catholic Church.

Of course, I happen to think one of those rituals is more efficacious than the other two. I'll leave you to guess which one. But, in every case, it's a form of prayer. It's also a form of meditation. We concentrate our whole selves—mind, body, and soul—on doing one true, good, and beautiful thing, and doing it perfectly.

Of course, not all rituals are religious. Not exactly. But all rituals are in some way meditative. Buddhist monks, who don't believe in a deity as such, will "paint" a stunning mandala with colored sand—and then the moment they're finished, they wipe it away.

Smoking a pipe is one of these secular rituals. Find yourself a comfortable chair on the porch, or a quiet road to walk down, either with a friend or all alone. Take out your pipe and pouch. Smell the shag. Fill the bowl and tamp it down gently. Light it once. Tamp it down again, and then light it a second time. Now sit or walk. Read or talk. Or just think.

The actual smoking requires a bit of concentration. Smoke it too slowly and it will get cold and the ashes will die. Smoke it too quickly and the ashes will get too hot and the stem will fill up with moisture; the smoke will turn ashy and sour.

But it won't take all of your attention, especially once you've had some practice. It only requires a little mindfulness. But that mindfulness is why the pipe enhances thinking or reading or conversation. It doesn't distract from it.

It's like the Rosary. One prays the Paternosters and Ave Marias while also meditating on the life of Christ. The prayers don't distract from the mysteries, because the human mind is always doing *at least* two things at once. The prayers and the mysteries focus both hemispheres of the brain on heavenly things.

So it is with the pipe. It keeps that "other part" of the mind from wandering off. It allows for total mindfulness. It eases us into that state of real patience.

That's why we say that cigarettes will do in a pinch. But a cigarette can be smoked quickly or slowly, and it makes no real difference to the quality of the smoke. There's a kind of mindfulness, but not much in the way of patience. And cigars are just disgusting.

Making tea is much the same way: it should be tied to patience and ritual. Acquire the following items: a tea kettle, a small teapot, a largeish tea infuser, a set of cups and saucers, and some loose tea. Those items won't break the bank, and they'll make the whole experience more enjoyable.

Feel free to experiment with your teas, because different teas require slightly different preparation. If you steep green tea at the same temperature as black tea, it will singe the leaves. If you steep black tea for as long as you steep herbal tea, it will go bitter.

When I make green tea, for instance, I carefully remove the top from the kettle once the water boils. I wait until there's just a wisp of steam coming off the water, and then pour it into the pot. Most sources will recommend you steep it for one minute; I find that forty-five seconds is ideal.

Don't be a snob, of course, but if you're making tea for yourself, it's good to be particular; that's how you develop tea-brewing skill. If your friend makes you a cup of tea, be gracious and enjoy it; if you're making tea for company, put your newly acquired skills to good use.

The pot and cup add to the ceremony, but they're also eminently practical. Tea stays hot for longer if you're only pouring out a little at a time.[3] But the rest is purely ritual.

Like smoking a pipe, making tea is a Patient Art—or it ought to be. Heating up a cup of water in the microwave and sticking a bag of Lipton in it is the equivalent of smoking a cigarette. It's fine, but since man is a creature of ritual, the goal should be to "ritualize" as much of his life as he possibly can. For, again, ritual is only doing one true, good, and beautiful thing, and doing it perfectly. Make every pipe you smoke the perfect pipe, and every cup of tea the perfect cup.

However, the consummate Patient Art is, of course, gardening.

Nearly everyone can garden. If you have a little bit of land around your house, it's astonishing how much you can grow: cucumbers, eggplants, raspberries—basically whatever you like. If you have enough land for an in-ground swimming pool, you can keep enough chickens that you never have to buy eggs again.

An acre or more is practically enough to live off of. You can grow pumpkins to sell at a farmer's market for a tidy profit at Halloween. And then you can also keep goats as well as chickens, which only need about as much pasture as a large garage, especially if you're supplementing their diet. Or plant a few apple trees and make your own ciders and pies.

Self-sufficiency is the medieval and the Nazarene ideal. There are any number of books that can teach one how to live off a single acre.[4] Homesteading is the consummation of the reactionary lifestyle. But even if you only live in an apartment, there's still plenty you can do. All cherry tomatoes need is a sunny windowsill and some dirt.

The point is to create something beautiful, something useful, and to keep tethered to the earth as best one can. Man was made for the Garden. Without a little dirt under his fingernails, he's like a fish out of water. And the first thing any gardener will tell you is that it really doesn't matter how small your yield is. I've seen men cradle their first cucumber like it was a newborn child. (Then they cut it up and put it in a gin and tonic.)

To work for months cultivating one plant, however small, and then to serve it to your friends and family is one of the few really universal pleasures in life. It's the most natural—the most human—of all pastimes. It's how we participate in the greatest ritual of all: the ceaseless unfolding of creation. When you hold that cherry tomato between your fingers, you know why God looked at the world and saw that it was good.

CHAPTER SEVENTEEN

Musings of a Human Liberationist

There is no sense and no sanity in objecting to the destruction of the flag while tolerating and justifying and encouraging as a daily business the desecration of the country for which it stands.
—Wendell Berry

I've met a few environmentalists in my day but, curiously, never outside. One usually finds them in lecture halls and television studios. They grow like weeds on Capitol Hill. Now and then you might come across one protesting in a big city, hemmed in on all sides by concrete, in the permanent shadow of skyscrapers, sandals flip-flopping on asphalt beneath a canopy of smog. But I'm not sure that really counts.

The kinds of people I've come across hiking, hunting, fishing, and camping are of a very different sort. They don't litter, but I don't think they recycle, either. They know what a Class VI road is, but they've never heard of the Kyoto Protocol. They know a half dozen ways to keep deer from eating their garden strawberries, but they'd laugh at anyone who used the phrase "Mother Earth."

Don't get me wrong: I think recycling is an excellent idea. But it doesn't seem to matter as much to outdoorsmen as it does to greenies—who are, for the most part, thoroughly "indoorsy."

True, environmentalists can rattle off a list of scientific studies that show the earth will burst into flames by 2050 unless we all go vegan. And they might be right. But their relationship with nature is purely transactional. Trees are things that give us air. We need to protect the trees, or else we won't have any air. And that's quite true! But one can't help but wonder if our environmentalist friends have ever seen a tree.

For those who've been privileged to spend their lives romping through the woods, as I have, the fact that trees produce air is practically the *last* thing we notice. A million poems have been written, and a million more are sure to be written, about the awesome sight of a gentle breeze setting these 20,000-pound titans to swaying like leaves of grass. The gnarled bark and knotty branches are like the skin of a man impossibly old and infinitely weathered, as if he'd sat down in a little plot of earth in the Bronze Age and resolved to stay put till Judgment Day. Every tree in every forest—100 billion trees in 100,000 forests—is like a cross between the Colossus of Rhodes and Rip Van Winkle. They're the most mystical of God's creations. If a man has seen a tree and doesn't believe in God, then—well, he hasn't seen a tree.

Going out into the woods doesn't make me want to reduce my carbon footprint. Maybe it should. But I'm not so morbid that I'm reminded of the destruction of the Amazon rainforest when I step into the Great North Woods. Usually, my mind is pretty fixed on the Great North Woods. In fact, at no other time would I feel so unsympathetic to the environmentalist's slogan, "Think Globally, Act Locally." I can't waste any time thinking about other people's woods. I'm perfectly absorbed in my own.

A man really can love humanity, but only if he figures out how to love his neighbor first. It's easy to love mankind in an abstract sort of way. Loving the bastard next door takes more practice. In just the same way, I doubt that anyone can truly learn to love trees unless he first learns to love *a* tree.

If you want a man to feel a certain horror at deforestation, make him think of *his* tree: the tree that held his swing or his fort when he was a boy, the tree with the weird hollow where he used to hide apples, the tree with the spindly branches where he shot his first squirrel, the tree under which he sat and read his first poem, the tree where he carved the name of his first love.

Otherwise, you have to scare him. Show him videos of starving polar bears floating on ice cubes off the coast of Canada. Tell him the avocado will go extinct unless we lower the global temperature by 1.8 degrees by next Wednesday. That will usually do the trick.

Well, not quite. Despite the constant klaxon being sounded by the United Nations, Hollywood celebrities, social media influencers, and other people whose opinions we're meant to care about for some reason, the vast majority of Americans don't seem especially panicked.

Maybe they don't understand what a difference that 1.8 degrees will make to an ecosystem. But how could they? You either believe the cryptic pronouncements of these scientific priests in white lab coats, or you don't. Climate science, like every other natural science, is a rarified field of contested theories. Today, alas, the government-academic-bureaucratic elite (who have intertwined financial interests) choose which theories they favor, and those theories are then presented to us by a credulous, politicized press as unassailable fact.

Really, I'm not saying that anthropogenic climate change is a lie—no more than I'm saying that God made the universe in six calendar days. I'm saying that I don't know one way or the other. True: many experts in climatology seem keen for us to outlaw cheeseburgers and to keep the levels of bovine flatus in the atmosphere under check. But experts in Scientology are equally keen to hook us into their E-meters so they can read our engrams or whatever. It's not obvious to me why I should believe one over the other.

Not to sound like a broken record, but this seems to me a perfect example of why the Enlightenment project of trying to ground policy in "facts" was doomed to fail—especially when applied to a mass democracy. If saving the planet depends on the majority of Americans' coming to understand climate science, then we are doomed. If it depends on a majority of *climate* scientists' truly understanding climate science, then we are all doomed. How much do you trust the weatherman?

That's why the Left's slogan isn't "Understand Science." It's "Believe Science." Believe in the dogmas handed down by the church of scientism. And its magisterial pronouncements go well beyond climate change. Of course, they tell us that man evolved from monkeys. Also, he can become a woman simply by *feeling* like one. "Not all women have wombs," they say. And those who do aren't capable of bearing human children, because babies only become human beings once they exit the birth canal. Before that, they're just a clump of cells that can be cut out and disposed of without hesitation.

I don't mean to belittle the progressives' faith in scientism. I just wish they could appreciate how bizarre all of this sounds to those of us who aren't paid-up members.

The deeper problem with environmentalism, however, is that it follows the same logic as consumerism. It sees the earth as a finite resource that we're burning through too quickly. And, in a sense, that's also quite true. But why should that matter to anyone?

It certainly shouldn't matter to progressives whose militant commitment to the pro-choice agenda has probably doomed their more noble commitment to protecting the planet. As the late, great Joe Sobran noted, abortion has abolished the "automatic coincidence of interest between parent and child":

Pro-choice rhetoric sends out a message that can only be translated as the right of parents to resent their children. If a child has no simple right to live before birth, will [a child have]...a right not to be abused afterward? Not if life itself is so cheap as that. The man or woman who regrettably waived the right to abort is not necessarily likely to regard the small child as a sacred trust.

Why should a progressive be concerned about her great-great-great-grandchildren dying in a global drought if she's not at all concerned about aborting her own children—and is perhaps even encouraging others to abort their children in the name of saving the planet? The Left wants us to preserve the planet for future generations, whom we might as well abort out of existence. Forgive me for saying this plainly, but the Catholic Church is far more logical in its sense of man's responsible stewardship over nature as God's creation than is the church of scientism, which wants man to save the planet for no particular reason at all.

That's also why outdoorsy people have always preferred conservationism to environmentalism. Conservation isn't a science: it's a romance. It's a defense of creation by those who love her most. The greatest conservationist in American history was, of course, Theodore Roosevelt, the big-game hunter who taxidermized his own trophies. His relationship with nature wasn't transactional. He didn't see the earth as a resource to be spent, wisely or not. He saw nature as a good *in itself.*[1] There was no question in his mind that it ought to be protected. You might as well have asked him if we shouldn't pull down Chartres Cathedral to make room for something more useful, such as a strip mall.

In 1886, Roosevelt ran for mayor of New York against our friend (and fellow reactionary) Henry George. Roosevelt was a Republican, of course, while George ran for the United Labor Party. Clearly, the two didn't see eye to eye on everything. But I suspect Teddy would have agreed with the basic principle of Georgism: that men can't really *own* the land. We didn't make it, and we have no title from its Maker. He didn't give it to us; he only lends it to us. We manage his property in his stead.[2]

For the record, we have no *jus abutendi* (the Roman law's recognition of an absolute right over property). We can't abuse the earth for our own pleasure. That wasn't part of the deal.

"The equal right of all men to the use of land is as clear as their equal right to breathe the air," George wrote. That certainly gets a bit tricky, of course, when you try to translate it into public policy. But Roosevelt made a good start by founding the U.S. Forest Service and expanding our National Parks. He believed that all Americans should, by virtue of their citizenship, be entitled to enjoy our natural treasures: the trees, the mountains, the lakes, the animals, the land.

Of course, the reactionary would go much further. He would seek to give each man his portion of the land to use (but not abuse) according to his needs. That was the medieval ideal. We're all called to be stewards of the earth, and that isn't an abstraction. It doesn't only mean refraining from throwing one's Taco Bell wrapper out the car window. It means each and every one of us ought to be planting trees and culling weeds. That is why distributists have taken for our slogan, "Three acres and a cow." True: it's mean fare, compared to what the average serf enjoyed. But it's a start.

Man was made for the Garden. Whatever his particular vocation, he will always be a gardener at heart. That's where he'll find his true happiness, his real satisfaction: on his knees, with the sun on his neck, his hands plunged into the dirt right up to the elbows.

At the very least, we can't have a real environmentalist movement when man is so divorced from nature. This is why the great conservatives were always conservationists and outdoorsmen. As soon as he made a little money, Russell Kirk moved back to his ancestral home in Mecosta, Michigan, where he planted thousands of trees. "There is nothing more conservative than conservation," he declared. (Kirk was also an admirer of Theodore Roosevelt, and it is telling that so many "conservatives" today are not because of Roosevelt's violation of libertarian orthodoxies.)

Likewise, in 1993, Sir Roger Scruton bought a hundred-acre farm, which he named "Scrutopia" and worked himself. "Conservatism and conservation are two aspects of a single long-term policy," Sir Roger declared, "which is that of husbanding resources and ensuring their renewal. These resources include the social capital embodied in laws, customs, and institutions; they also include the material contained in the environment."

He wondered aloud why environmentalists didn't have more sympathy for conservatives. After all, the two are "both in search of the motives that will defend a shared but threatened legacy from predation by its current trustees."

Kirk and Scruton both belonged to the traditionalist faction of Anglo-American conservatism. At its best, traditionalism is a gateway to reaction; traditionalists are allies against not only the Left but against the official, GOP-sanctioned, think tank–led Conservative Movement™ that long ago put the trads into a kind of ghetto.

Traditionalists are allowed, even encouraged, to talk about conservative principles in the abstract, but they may never challenge the consumer-capitalist-globalist consensus of free markets, free trade, and foreign policy internationalism, even when policies excused under these guises undercut American workers, American families, American traditions, and American national interests. This is the insanity of modern conservatism, and explains why the allegedly conservative Republican Party so often seems like a slower, stodgier version of the Democratic Party, interested only in tweaking and slowing the Democrats' agenda to better protect the Chamber of Commerce.

Conservationism is only one more example of this same, sad predicament. Unless we can convince conservatives that endless consumption and economic growth are not the chief measures of a healthy society, we won't convince them of the need for conservation. Unfortunately, endless consumption and economic growth is the whole *raison d'être* of modern conservatism (and liberalism, by the way; it just favors different economic sectors).

Wendell Berry noted, "The desecration of nature would have been impossible without the desecration of work, and vice versa," by which he meant that we can't save the environment without returning to an economy of farmers and craftsmen, an economy on a smaller, more human scale.

Certainly, the invisible hand of the market will never convince us to stop cutting down trees, unless it's for the sake of giving some billionaire a nice view of the park from his New York penthouse. It will never convince us to stop polluting the oceans, unless it's the little strip of sea outside the tycoon's beach house in Florida. The market commodifies everything. That's its job. And, in its workings, it has turned nature itself into a luxury good.

Remember what Henry George said: "The equal right of all men to the use of land is as clear as their equal right to breathe the air." He wouldn't have been surprised to learn that, in China, the rape of the land has thrown up so much smog that denizens of Beijing are buying cans of fresh air from Canada. Who can honestly call that "progress"?

The most important argument for conservation is that nature is good, as God made it. Man is also good, as God made him. It is understandable, perhaps, that an atheist society such as Communist

China would deny God, deny the goodness of man (limiting him to one child and putting him under Communist Party control), and deny the goodness of nature (which is meant to be exploited by materialist man). What is odder, perhaps, is that this attitude has become prevalent in America. But if we take such a cold, transactional view of our fellow man as to say it's okay to kill unborn babies and euthanize old people, how can we convince people to respect plant and animal life, short of erecting a new religion that puts plants and animals above ourselves?

This is the final frontier of consumerism. It's why I say progressives are fundamentally capitalists, and capitalists will always tend to become progressives. (You see this, incidentally, in every "conservative" who says he is fiscally conservative and socially liberal; he always eventually comes out as a liberal, full stop.) Capitalist conservatives and socialist or crony-capitalist liberals are united in putting economics, commercialism, and materialism at the core of society, and yet few realize the extent to which modern man has commercialized everything, most especially including nature.

I can *almost* approve of vegetarians who boycott meat to protest the cruelty of corporate slaughterhouses. But you'll catch the vegetarian's error right away if you listen to his slogans closely enough. He'll say something like, "We keep these animals in conditions that are nothing less than inhumane." Which is quite true! But—and this will come as a shock to many, many people—animals *aren't* humans. We don't need to keep them in *humane* conditions. We need to keep them in *animal* conditions—that is, conditions that respect their dignity as animals, as fellow creatures. But that doesn't mean we have to put them up at the Ritz.

It's always the indoorsy people who say things like, "I love animals so much! I could never kill them for food when I can get by on a nice bowl of quinoa." If they spent any amount of time in nature with wild animals, they'd see that animals kill each other for food all the time. Really, they don't mind. A vegetarian's pet dog certainly wouldn't mind eating meat—or killing the neighboring farmer's chickens.

Vegetarians—and brutal corporate slaughterhouses—are only possible when normal citizens are completely divorced from their food supply. Human herbivores were rare when most people had hunted a deer, bled a pig, or deboned a fish. It's not always a pleasant experience, but it's humbling. It feels natural. You quickly locate yourself within the animal kingdom.

You also get a feeling of profound gratitude for this fellow creature which gave its lifeblood for your sake. The staunchest atheist will find himself wanting to kneel beside the animal like an Iroquois and offer it a prayer of thanksgiving. The animal takes on a nobility that one couldn't have really imagined otherwise. There's an unmistakable sense that your fate is bound to the fate of this creature in a way that it can never be bound to (say) your mailman or your dentist.

This feeling of gratitude is what separates man from our fellow predators, such as lions and tigers and bears. While vegetarians might *like* animals a whole lot, nobody can really claim to love animals unless he's killed one. That's the strange, wonderful paradox of the human creature. By embracing our animal nature, we transcend it.

Nothing displays our disordered view of nature more than the way we treat "house pets" as humans (often, in this infertile age, they take the place of children). We keep them pent up in our houses and apartments all day. We regulate when they can go outside to walk (seldom to run) and when to excrete waste. We "let" them sleep at the foot of our beds. Some of us even make them compete in dog shows, which are only slightly less demeaning than beauty pageants. And we say we *love* them.

Let me break the news to you: I'm sure your dog likes you well enough, but he doesn't want to live with you. He doesn't want to be your pet. He wants to be a dog, and he wants to live with other dogs. He doesn't want to wear clothes; he's happy with the fur that God gave him. He wants to hunt for his own food, and to eat it right off the bone, as God intended. He wants to relieve himself on God's green earth whenever the spirit moves him. He wants to walk when he feels like it, run when he feels like it, sit when he feels like it, and stay when he feels like it. He wants to sniff every leaf and pee on every tree. And he wants to sleep in a cave with a pile of other dogs, warm and snug and safe.

You may be shocked. You may not even believe me. But I'm telling you the truth. Your dog doesn't want to be treated "humanely." He wants to be treated dogly. He wants to be treated like a dog, not a human. Because he's not a human. He's a dog.

Dogs aren't like other domesticated animals. Cows want a patch of grass to eat and a little shade under a tree. Humans can provide that much. If we protect them from wolves and coyotes, so much the better. It's the same with chickens. They don't mind living in a coop, provided they have a little room to flap their wings. They can still live their best chickeny lives. It doesn't bother them overmuch. But dogs don't want to wear sweaters or eat kibble or sleep on feather beds.

Now, there *is* a way to domesticate dogs humanely—or, rather, dogly. Lots of hunters will keep a whole pack of hounds in their backyards. They're free to run around as much as they like. They sleep together in some wooden shelter, as a pack. And they're given plenty of opportunities to stalk and kill prey. But that's the best, and perhaps the *only*, example of humans and dogs living together and working for their common good.

Then, of course, there's the horror of the toy dogs. Anyone who really admires dogs must be horrified by the fact that we've created dozens of these breeds, which were genetically engineered to be as small and useless as possible.

It's no accident that lapdogs and toy breeds arose from the immediate post-feudal era, when Europe's aristocracy became divorced from its proper function. As landowners became increasingly ostracized from the land, they came to favor dogs that were completely stripped of their dogness, purely decorative canines for a purely decorative elite.

It's not my intention to disparage all dog owners; it's fine to breed dogs for some *useful* purpose that fits their nature: Golden Retrievers are happy to have pheasants to retrieve; sheepdogs are happy to herd sheep; and humans and dogs really can love one another when they live and work side by side.

But that's quite different from carrying around a shivering Chihuahua in one's handbag. We don't show our love for something by exploiting it for our amusement. That goes for dogs as well as people.

I believe in free-range men who run through green pastures, swim in clear waters, and breathe fresh mountain air. And I believe that a man who is right with nature won't abuse animals; he'll live among them, work alongside them, and, yes, eat them occasionally—and learn to love them again.

CHAPTER EIGHTEEN

The Strenuous Life

He had the gaunt and haunted athletic look of those who stare daily down the bony gullet of the great god Aerobics.

—Tom Wolfe

T he great English radical (and reactionary) William Cobbett advocated many reforms, but perhaps none more important than the return of Englishmen to the three Bs of an old English breakfast: bread, bacon, and beer. Before the East India Company introduced tea to the British public in the seventeenth century, no self-respecting Englishman would begin the day without a flagon of ale. It kept him fit, warm, and full through a long day tilling the fields.

The true reactionary today would return to this wholesome and healthful practice.

Yet, in this, we may be alone. The ideal of health—of being hale and hearty—has disappeared. Men lost their health when they lost their meaningful work on the land, which also cost them their freedom and independence. Today they settle for little things like "fitness" and (God help us) "wellness."

Take, for instance, the rise of the gymnasium. Of all the institutions that blight our landscape—factories, public schools, fast-food restaurants, strip malls, banks, and all the rest—the gym must be the most invidious.

Gyms have been forces of evil since their inception. Their modern form was invented in the early nineteenth century by Friedrich Ludwig Jahn, an important forerunner to Hitlerism. Jahn was a racist, an anti-Semite, and an enemy of the German crown; he was a "liberal" who was also (surprise) a firm believer in authoritarian rule. The Nazis themselves acknowledged their debt to him; the ideologue Alfred Baeumler wrote, "Only the overthrow of the nineteenth century by National Socialism has enabled us to see freely and purely the figure of Jahn."

But Jahn's contribution wasn't principally intellectual. It was the creation of these gymnasiums. His gymnasts, who were mostly middle-class students, exulted in a cult of raw power and brute strength. Young gymnasts organized themselves into gangs, calling themselves "stormtroopers" and menacing folks on the street who looked insufficiently German.

Gyms, then, were the consummation of what early reactionaries referred to as "Prussianism." They fostered a culture of militarism, which saw war—the exercise of mass violence—as a positive good rather than a necessary evil. This Prussianism was the primary cause of World War I and was revived by Hitler as a means of organizing Germany for what became World War II.

As Jahn's gymnasiums popped up at colleges across the German-speaking world, they also spread Jahn's radical ideology—and the political violence which attended it. "The gymnastic institution is the real training ground for the university mischief," Prince Klemens von Metternich rightly observed. "One has to grasp the evil by the roots."

Of course, there's nothing wrong with strength. Men should be strong. In fact, for most of human history, there was no opportunity for men *not* to be strong. Farmers, stonemasons, blacksmiths—one couldn't make a living without putting muscle on one's bones. But they came by that muscle the honest way, by working hard and doing useful things. They had neither the time nor the need for a gym. It was only in a bourgeois society like nineteenth-century Germany that students, divorced from any real work, could supplement their idle studies with idle exercises.

The gymnasts aspired to the strength of the common man but refused to share in his labors. That was beneath them. They were intellectuals. They couldn't afford to waste their muscles on tilling soil or building churches. Their exercise, like their education, had to be ordered towards politics. Their minds and their bodies had to be focused entirely towards their wicked ideology.

The gym is, in fact, an ideological tool. And so all those who reject ideology must absolutely reject the gymnasium.

I know that many conservatives, and even many reactionaries, are today great advocates of the gym. They see it as a means of counteracting the softening and effeminization of men. And I don't mean to insult them. Not in the least bit. Their instincts are basically sound. But in this instance, gyms are only a kind of placebo. They trick men into thinking that they can make up for real *work* simply by lifting heavy things. These toy muscles are to real strength what hook-up culture is to spousal love. It's a lousy substitute, yes. But it's one that we can easily deceive ourselves into thinking is good enough, at least for our intents and purposes.

If men didn't have gyms, they might very well go soft. But, more likely, they would revolt. They would revolt against the socio-economic order that has deprived them of real, meaningful work. They would demand we return to when a man earned his bread by exercising both mind and body—as a farmer, a stonemason, a blacksmith, a soldier (a knight), or what have you.

As with the original gymnasts, "fitness" today has become an ideological exercise. When men were strong as a matter of course, they used that strength to make things that they, their family, their friends, and their neighbors needed—whether it was a field of potatoes or a wall or a horseshoe.

When strength is pursued as its own end—even with the best of intentions, and by the best of people—it ceases to be a matter of utility and charity; it becomes an act of vanity.

And here we come to the really absurd thing. As gymnasiums have been stripped of their Prussianism, the gymnast has ceased even to be a stormtrooper. He's become a gym bunny, proud of his grotesquely swollen limbs.

I know most reactionaries who go to the gym don't feel this way, but it's certainly the case with almost everyone else who lifts weights as a hobby, conservative or otherwise. Their muscles have nothing to do with being useful, or even strong. It's only about impressing girls—and, more usually, other guys. As the excellent Lara Prendergast wrote in *The Spectator* a few years ago, "Nowadays, male self-improvement is all the rage and men are now almost as boring about their appearance as women."

What the best of them are *really* after is the strenuous life. Our friend Teddy Roosevelt coined the phrase in one of his greatest speeches, where he declared:

> A life of ignoble ease, a life of that peace which springs merely from lack either of desire or of power to strive after great things, is as little worthy of a nation as of an individual.... We do not admire the man of timid peace. We admire the man who embodies victorious effort; the man who never wrongs his neighbor, who is prompt to help a friend, but who has those virile qualities necessary to win in the stern strife of actual life.

That's the difference between fitness and health, between toy muscles and real strength. When I was growing up, one of my fellow farmhands, Bill, used to help an old man down the road collect his hay. Bill could spend an hour throwing hay bales from the ground to the barn loft—over one vertical story—without stopping to rest. He stood at about five foot five and probably weighed 150 pounds. I haven't met many stronger men, and those that were were a lot bigger—and farmers.

Bill lived the strenuous life. He was strong, and he used his strength to help his neighbors. His biceps didn't bulge out of his shirt. It was all lean, practical muscle, like Teddy's.

When Roosevelt gave his speech, he was addressing a nation that was already thoroughly bourgeois, and whose working class was thoroughly "proletarianized." For the first time, masses of freemen were being shackled to office chairs or stationed before conveyor belts. They had no creative outlet, physical or intellectual. Roosevelt recognized that something was going terribly wrong in American society. The "strain" of real hard work done by farmers and craftsmen had played an outsized role in making this country great. And, suddenly, it was gone.

Despite their considerable differences, Teddy was in touch with the best of the Jeffersonian tradition. Like Jefferson, he believed that the basis of a strong civil society was the rugged individual. The yeoman farmer, the minuteman, is precisely the fellow whom Teddy extolled—the one "who does not shrink from danger, from hardship, or from bitter toil, and who out of these wins the splendid ultimate triumph." Without this noble strain, he becomes nothing more than "a cumberer of the earth's surface," though he may be an especially muscular cumberer.

The reactionary ideal, of course, is that honest work should be restored to humanity. The first rule of thumb is to go outside. Another great evil of gyms is that it divorces exercise from the outdoors. You'd do more for your health by walking in a park for twenty minutes than by lifting dumbbells in a gym for an hour. Fresh air, as our mothers knew, is the ultimate cure-all. Man is an animal—and, like any animal, he needs dirt between his toes and the sun on his back.

Also, if you're a man, get punched in the face at some point in your life. That's one experience every man should have, without exception; it teaches humility and reality. A lot of my boxer friends feel a certain horror at the idea of bare-knuckle fighting. They associate it with mixed martial arts—which, admittedly, isn't the most elegant sport. But, for single men, there's nothing wrong with having a few beers, going out in the backyard, and throwing hands.

We all live such comfortable, sheltered lives that we can never imagine calling on our friends to protect us. But that wasn't the case back in the day, when army regiments were recruited from the same state, and even the same town. The assumption was that all those boys had traded blows at some point.

Still, even today, all male friendship is based on the (usually unconscious) faith that, if your back is against the wall, your true friends would step up and fight alongside you. If you think your drinking buddy is a coward, or that he can't hold his own, you're not going to respect him. It doesn't matter how much you like him. It doesn't matter if he can spin a good yarn or carry a tune. If you don't trust him to see you out of a pinch, there will always be a gap between you.

Some of my closest friendships were forged over a friendly brawl. I promise you, there's no harm in it. Have at it until it stops being fun, and then bow out. A few weeks later, go again. As long as the loser is gracious and the winner is magnanimous, you'll both have a great time. You'll respect your brothers that much more, and they you.

This might sound barbaric to the average reader. We have this great societal horror of violence. Yet we think nothing of the fact that young men spend all their free time playing *Grand Theft Auto* or *Call of Duty*.

Look: the problem isn't violence. Violence is a normal part of life. That's not going away. The problem is that we dissociate violence from its natural consequences. It's like the "online disinhibition effect" writ large. We're more apt to be cruel in real life when we have no sense of how our cruelty might harm other people—other living, breathing human beings.

Men who know how to throw a punch—and what it feels like to get hit—have a healthy respect for violence. There's a reason why Antifa goons attack in packs, like hyenas. It's because they glorify violence in an abstract way. They love the idea of spraying mace into the eyes of a "fascist" and then kicking him, stomping him, and punching him when he's vulnerable and little threat to themselves. You get the impression they were trained on video games, not school-yard tussles.

So, get it out of your system. Punch your friend, and have him punch you. You'll both be better men for it.

Speaking of violence, hunting is another great way to get outside and exercise body and wit—as Teddy would attest. If you can't hunt deer or turkey, hunt squirrel or rabbit. A professional once told me that shooting small game is the best way to hone your marksmanship. If you hit something, be sure to eat it. Squirrels and rabbits don't yield much meat, but they're abundant and can be found on any reasonably large piece of property. Rabbit stew is delicious, and so is fried squirrel.

Ideally, one should go hunting with other guys. Except for fighting, nothing cements a male friendship like spending a day walking through the woods, tripping over branches, drinking whiskey out of a flask, and shooting animals with guns. My grandfather, who taught me to hunt, once said to me: "Do you know how I know we're pals? Because we can spend a whole day together, not saying a word, and be perfectly happy." Any fellow hunter would know exactly what he meant.

A nun who taught at a girls' school explained to me that, as a father, when my daughter wants to talk, I should just shut up and listen. That's how women process things, she said. They think out loud. Well, men aren't like that. But the good news is that shutting up and listening is about 99 percent of hunting.

Hunting is also eminently useful. You can easily get fifty pounds of meat from an average-sized deer. If you figure half a pound of meat is more than enough for one meal, that's one hundred meals. It's a pretty good feeling, being able to bring home that much chow, and having a great time doing it. That's how men are supposed to live.

Fishing is a close second. We could easily file it away under the Patient Arts. It's generally more of a beer than a whiskey sport, but the idea is more or less the same.[1]

Presumably, most folks fish in lakes and rivers. I grew up by the ocean, so I can't really enjoy anything else. Waking up before the sun rises, pulling on your sweater and rain slicker, pushing the boat off the dock, gripping a hot cup of coffee poured from a thermos, feeling the cold salt air and the sea spray against your face as you peel away from the coast, looking behind you and seeing the coast has disappeared, being entirely alone on the wide ocean. You might be ten miles from home, but when it's just you and the sea, you might as well be square in the middle of the Atlantic.

But lakes are probably fun, too.

If you can do nothing else, go rucking. Rucking is walking while carrying a heavy backpack—usually about twenty pounds. One of my favorite exercises is rucking on wooded trails.

If you're stuck in a city or a suburb... well, get out, by any means necessary. But if you can't, ruck down the sidewalk. Just be sure to get outside, every day.

And remember: ruck, don't run. In his book *The Restoration of Christian Culture*, John Senior—one of the great reactionaries of our time—rightly urges us to "quit the absurd and unhealthy exhibitionism of jogging." Rucking is just as good for your heart and lungs, and it won't kill your knees. You need those if you're going to do more productive things, such as picking peas or praying.

Whatever you do, take cold showers. I can't tell you what a life-changing habit this is. It's like drinking three cups of coffee in three minutes, only there's no crash. It gets your mind and your blood racing all at once. Sloth will be out of the question.

Really, it makes perfect sense. Human beings are animals, and all animals are wired to respond to their environment. If our environment rapidly becomes colder, our body figures that it needs to prepare for hardship. Take a cold shower and you'll have all the energy, focus, and drive you'd need to chase down an elk. Believe me: if you have to choose between *that* and a grande mochaccino from Starbucks, go with the shower. Every time.

In 1849, Thomas Francis Meagher was exiled to Australia for participating in the Young Ireland uprising. But that didn't matter. He put his exile to good use. He'd trek through the bush, carrying huge stones on his back. He grew strong, lean, and tan. Eventually, he escaped Australia; less than a decade later, he was appointed brigadier general in the Union Army, commanding the Irish Brigade in the American Civil War.

My grandmother always said that we're related to Meagher somehow. I don't know if there's any truth to the story, but he looms large in family lore. He was a brilliant orator, soldier, athlete, and patriot. No man except old Teddy so perfectly embodied the strenuous life. Teddy, and my old neighbor Bill.

The Coming Dark Age

Happiness is not only a hope, but also in some strange manner a memory... we are all kings in exile.

—G. K. Chesterton

I t must have seemed odd to the Roman people that, while barbarians were systematically dismantling the empire, Augustine—the bishop of Hippo, renowned for his brilliance and holiness—was writing a book called *The City of God*.

But, really, nothing could be more sensible. When the world is falling apart around you, what can you do but turn your gaze to heaven?

Augustine wasn't a quietist. On the contrary, he was one of the first real political philosophers in the Christian tradition. He knew that government had its uses: to protect the poor, to keep the peace, and to foster virtue through just laws. But he also knew enough history to know that all governments reach a point of decay where they can no longer be saved, and that our only salvation is in God. "Christ is our Liberator," he declared, "insofar as he is our Savior."

I don't know if America has passed the point of no return. I suspect that it has. But that doesn't matter. The United States may survive for another ten thousand years, or it may fall apart tomorrow. But there comes a time when civilizations, no less than men, have to die.

To say so isn't impious. It isn't unpatriotic. One can love one's country while recognizing that it must, inevitably, die. We love our mothers all the more when we realize they won't be around forever. Thinking about death reminds us that we can take nothing for granted. And then we turn our gaze to heaven.

But Americans don't like to think about death. That's why we hide it away in hospitals and nursing homes. We buy our meat slaughtered and packaged, ready to go right in the oven. In war, we outsource our killing to drones, so that we can take a hundred men's lives without ever looking in their faces. When the state executes a man, it doesn't march him to a gallows in the public square. It kills him in a windowless room. It doesn't even give him the dignity of a bullet: just a few injections in the arm, as if it were a flu shot. It's much worse for the condemned, but much easier for the men who've condemned him.

Yet a people who can't confront mortality can't really be happy. They can only spend their lives hiding from death. They use drugs and alcohol to dampen their thoughts. They play video games in which players always respawn after flying through the windshield at a hundred miles an hour or having their heads blown off by a sniper rifle. They gape at screens, with their constant, endless flow of distracting lights and sounds. They shop for trinkets on the internet, hiding themselves in great igloos of worthless baubles. They have casual sex with perfect strangers, giving each other a brief escape from their loneliness. And we invent all kinds of clever procedures that prolong our natural lifespan, keeping the body alive even as the brain dies. We survive longer, yet we never really live.

That, I think, has always been the appeal of the Middle Ages. Some scholars like to say that man invented religion to quell his fear of death. The intense religiosity of the medieval serf was a way of escaping the endless cycle of famine and war and disease.

Really, I think it's just the opposite. Man can't really live if he spends his life running away from death. But when he keeps the veil that stands between life and death before his eyes, he can just make out the light shining behind it. Men used to believe that stars were only holes in the firmament, offering a glimpse of heaven's brightness in the night sky. And they were more right than wrong.

The whole of the modern world is designed to keep us from thinking about death. That is to say, it keeps us from living. This is the essence of progress: the extension, the softening, of our mortal existence at the expense of all else—of Truth, Goodness, Beauty, of family, friendship, and community, of peace and quiet, of work and leisure, of nature, of valor and sacrifice and love.

That isn't a fair trade.

Have we defined "reactionary" yet? If not, let's do so now. A reactionary is one who rejects the cheapness, the artificiality, of modern life. He demands the right to pursue his own happiness, and he refuses to accept mere comfort instead. He doesn't want to survive; he wants to live. And he wants to go to heaven.

That was the whole point of Christendom. Its sole purpose was to teach men how to live well and then go to heaven. All of the artifacts—the poems, the paintings, the music, the spires, the bells—weren't merely curios to distract man from death. We know what those look like. They're small and plastic and say "Made in China" on the bottom. No: they were offerings of gratitude to God, who gives us life and salvation. They didn't deny death. They affirmed life. They were acts not of fear or desperation, but of joy.

We Christians seem to have forgotten that. We've mistaken the form of Christendom for its substance. Some, such as Malcolm Muggeridge, hail the fall of Christendom (or "political Christianity") as an opportunity for spiritual renewal. Others, such as today's Christian conservatives—the religious Right—would preserve the political infrastructure of Christianity even if it means fostering hostility with our progressive and secular countrymen.

Both are wrong.

Muggeridge (whom I admire immensely) was wrong because Christendom, for all its failings, was basically a good thing. It was better than what came before, and it's certainly better than what's come after. It was more beautiful, more just, and more free. The Church will survive its death, but it was right that all laws and customs should have pointed to Christianity: the source of all beauty, justice, and freedom.

But the religious Right is wrong for just the opposite reason. When the population has ceased to believe in Christianity, the political infrastructure is worthless. Well, not worthless, exactly. Conservatives know that laws ought to define marriage as being between one man and one woman, for life. They know that gay marriage isn't laudable; in fact, it's not even marriage. They know that abortion is wrong. They know that transgenderism is insanity. But until our countrymen return in large numbers to Christianity, it seems unlikely that these laws will change in any meaningful way. We need to put the emphasis on religious conversion first before we can hope for any sort of political restoration.

And when it comes to conversion, we're doing a pretty bad job, aren't we? The peoples of the West are leaving the pews in droves. Whom do we blame if not ourselves? Are we not our brothers' keepers?

Christendom—a Christian society and culture, reflected in life and law—may be dead beyond any hope of resurrection. The American republic may fall. It may be succeeded by some techno-oligarchic tyranny, or it may be swept into the sea by a Chinese invasion. The whole industrial capitalist system may collapse and plunge our nation into anarchy, hunger, and war. Christians may once again become an openly persecuted sect. We may very well be headed for a new Dark Age.

If so, what then? What should our strategy be?

Well, our strategy should always be the same. Whether Christians are a majority or a minority, whether we're in power or hiding in the catacombs, we should be striving to turn men's hearts to Jesus Christ.

Yes, argue for just laws. We should fight for the common good. But politics is only supposed to amount to a tiny fraction of our public life.[1] Instead, it has swallowed us completely. Rather, as Saint Paul says, we should "avoid stupid controversies" and "quarrels over the law, for they are unprofitable and futile."

In all things, be kind. Again, we have the words of Saint Paul: "So, whether you eat or drink, or whatever you do, do all to the glory of God. Give no offense to Jews or to Greeks or to the church of God, just as I try to please all men in everything I do, not seeking my own advantage, but that of many, that they may be saved."

If we really love our fellow man, then it will show in everything we do. We should, in the words of Saint Paul, "do what is good." Give food to the hungry and drink to the thirsty. Welcome the stranger. Clothe the naked. Visit the sick and imprisoned, the orphans and widows. "Let no evil talk come out of your mouths, but only such as is good for edifying, as fits the occasion, that it may impart grace to those who hear." Above all, "love the Lord your God with all your heart, and with all your soul, and with all your mind, and with all your strength," and "love your neighbor as yourself."

That's the best that any man can do. I keep coming back to a magnificent little book by the French philosopher Charles Péguy called *Temporal and Eternal.* In it, Péguy says that "the politically minded... think they can save themselves, by saying that they are at least practical, and that we are not." Alas:

That is precisely where they are mistaken. Where they mislead. We do not even grant them that. It is the mystic who is practical, and the politically minded who are not. It is we who are practical, *who do something*, and it is they who are not, *who do nothing*. It is we who accumulate and they who squander. It is we who build, lay foundations, and they who demolish. It is we who nourish, and they who are parasites. It is we who make things and men, people and races. It is they who wreak ruin.

Christendom only ever existed because it was built on a solid foundation of charity, active charity: men and women doing what was good. It gave credibility to Christianity's claims. The peoples of pagan Europe believed that Christians weren't just trying to advance their cult. They believed we had something good to share with the world. That's because we *did*. And we still do today. Christian charity is the best means for Christian conversion.

Beyond that, we can build up our Christian communities. I'm a great admirer of Rod Dreher's book *The Benedict Option*. To elaborate further on the community-building aspect would be pointless, since Mr. Dreher has basically said all that needs to be said on the subject. Please, forget everything you've heard about it being "retreatist." That's a lie. It's a lie that sprang from the fevered minds of men who can't imagine life outside of politics. Mr. Dreher is one of the real prophets of our time, and his advice on this point should be heeded urgently.

Above all, though, be happy. Live well, and go to heaven. If you can do nothing else, do that. The reactionary is one whose whole existence is a constant revolt against the modern world—its banal, cheap, ugly, heartless futility.

Fall in love, get married, and be faithful to your spouse. Have as many children as you possibly can. Your family will bring you more joy than anything else in the world. It's worth every sacrifice you make, of which there will be many.

Homeschool your kids, but don't over-school them. Let them pay a little more attention to topics that interest them. Let them take long lunches. End their studies while there's still daylight so they can play outside. Start or join a co-op so they can be around other children of all ages.

Build a community. Find a parish that will nourish your faith. Make friends who will strengthen you in virtue. Have fun together. Exercise together—mind, body, and soul. Sing good songs. Read good books. Start a branch of the Chesterton Society or a smial of the Tolkien Society. Hunt, fish, and hike. Drink beer. Smoke pipes. Laugh.

Stay away from cities. Cities are where souls go to die. Extricate yourself from the ugliness of modern life as best you can. Go out into the country. Go up into the mountains.

Don't worry too much about your career. Your priority should be keeping your family fed. But, if you can, find a useful occupation. Farm. Make furniture. Unclog toilets. If you're doomed to a life of white-collar labor, try to find a job that lets you work from home. Minimize your commute. Never take a promotion that forces you to move away from your community.

If you can't buy a farm, plant a garden. Spend a little time every day with your hands in the soil. Eat fruits and vegetables you've grown yourself. Raise chickens and eat their eggs. If you can, buy a few goats or cows. Keep your family in good, raw milk. At least once in your life, go in on a pig with some friends and slaughter it yourselves.

Minimize the amount of technology you use for work. Don't use any technology recreationally. Avoid social media like the plague. Never read the comments on an article. Remember that nobody in the history of the world has ever changed his mind after arguing with a stranger online. Get a dumbphone or a landline to keep in touch with friends and family, but find better things to do with your free time. Practice real leisure. Learn to play an instrument. Paint. Whittle. Write poetry. Play chess. Be strenuous, and be useful.

Throw away your television. Turn off the talk radio. Get your news from a local newspaper. Better yet, don't get the news at all. If the country goes to war, you'll hear about it. Otherwise, it's none of your business, and nobody cares what you think.

When you go out in public, put on a tie. It doesn't matter whom you're going to see: they're worth it. Comport yourself with dignity, and with respect for the dignity of others. You wouldn't throw rubbish in your front yard for all your neighbors to see. So, don't go outside looking like a slob. They deserve better. So do you. And so does your family. A true reactionary wears a tie at home.

Buy a few dogs and work alongside them. Find a sense of purpose together. Let them retrieve the birds you shoot and watch over your livestock. Then, let them run around and play together.

Shop local. If you can't buy it locally, 99 percent of the time you don't need it. Spend less money, period. Don't create waste. Recycle and compost. Don't throw clothes away; patch them.

Washington is a lost cause. It's the seat of a dying empire. Get involved in local politics. Register as an independent and work with politicians of any party to build the common good. Use prudence, of course. Never vote for a "pro-choice" politician who could feasibly change abortion law in a "liberal" direction. But if the Democrat running for city council wants to plant a thousand trees and the

Republican wants to tear down a park to build a strip mall, vote for the Democrat. For larger executive offices, such as mayor or governor, remember that you're not just electing a man (or woman), but an administration, and vote accordingly for the administration that would do the least harm through executive orders and appointments.

Go to church (or synagogue or whatever your house of worship happens to be) once a week. If you're Catholic, go to daily Mass. Lead your family in prayer every evening. Tithe: give 10 percent of your income to your church, a religious order, or to worthy, reactionary causes. Don't get dragged into "church politics"—local, national, or international. It will kill your faith at its roots. Just focus on what you can do, personally, to spread your faith.

Examine your conscience every evening. Don't be afraid to confront your sins or your mortality. Be brave. Think about them, but not too much. Make it your resolve every night to be a better man the next morning, and then do that.

This is how the reactionary wages his war against modernity—with his whole being. He doesn't depend on new-fangled things such as parties or "movements." He has no use for factions or sects. By definition, one party or faction must defeat the other. That's the point. The reactionary isn't interested in beating his opponents, but in winning them over. He has something that they need, and he wants to share it with them: happiness. A good life. Reactionaries don't argue; they act. They lead by example.

This is the reactionary imperative. We say that his whole existence is an act of defiance, and so it is. But it's also an invitation. It's an invitation to adopt his convictions, to practice his virtues, and to share in his happiness. The truth is that we *know* our way is better. We know that men can only find satisfaction by being simple, kind, pious, and good. And we prove that not through debates or newspaper columns, but by living "loyally and joyfully."

This is the right thing to do. It also happens to be the most expedient. Listen: the huge majority of men who are converted to a certain belief system—Christianity, Islam, communism, hedonism, whatever—aren't motivated by sound reasoning. As Cardinal Newman said, "It is as absurd to argue men, as to torture them, into believing." I've met hundreds of converts to the Catholic Church in my career as a Catholic journalist, and only one of them was won over by reading the *Summa*. None of them were won over by some congressional bill supported by the Heritage Foundation.

Some were struck by the beauty of a cathedral or an old hymn. Others found the poetry of T. S. Eliot or the novels of J. R. R. Tolkien. Many were charmed by the simple apologetics of laymen such as Chesterton or Lewis. Others heard the preaching of a joyful Catholic priest or were helped in their lives by a gentle Catholic nun. A few, like me, had a "Road to Damascus" moment, where they directly experienced God's irresistible grace.

The vast majority, however, had some encounter with a happy Catholic family. They stumbled into a wholesome Catholic "intentional community," like our little clan here in New Hampshire. They saw big families laughing and singing and praying together. These families don't usually bring home big paychecks. Their communities don't have much sway in the statehouse. You're not going to see them profiled on Fox News.

They live lives of simple piety and quiet charity. The men like hard work, good beer, and guns. The women like babies, crafts, and dresses. The children like playing in the mud, skinning their knees, and reading stories about knights saving damsels from dragons.

If you've ever met these folks, you know exactly what I mean. They make you say to yourself, "This is how I want to live. This is how I want to be. I want to be part of this... this *thing* they have going on here. Their way is better than my way."

Let me say again: this is a book about happiness, not hedonism. Once you enter into these communities, you realize pretty quickly that the way of tradition is much harder than the modern cult of comfort. As John of the Cross wrote in *The Dark Night of the Soul*, those who would reach the summit of happiness must walk the path of sorrows.

But it's worth it. And nobody who's walked that path will deny it. Nobody who's seen a Franciscan friar eating a sandwich with a drug addict on the streets of Detroit, or watched the Bruderhof brethren singing "Come to the Woods" as they haul bushels of carrots across the frozen earth, will deny it. They have something the rest of us have lost. They do what is good.

If the Right has a future, this is it. If the *world* has a future, this is it. It won't be the politicians, think-tankers, journalists, economists, and philanthropists who save the world. It will be the everyday mystics, such as these folks. It will be the reactionaries who have kept the faith alive.

Anthony Burgess once said, "I suppose my conservatism, since the idea of a Catholic Jacobite imperial monarch isn't practical, is really a kind of anarchism." That's fine. The reactionary, being adverse to ideology, can travel under a variety of labels: anarcho-monarchism, neo-feudalism, paleo-fogeyism, Southern Agrarianism, or Robert Frost's northern version. I don't care. We all get the idea.

This isn't a manifesto. It's an invitation to imagine a better future, which begins by imagining a better past. Don't wait for a groundswell of popular opinion. Don't wait for a party or a faction or a movement. I promise you, the counter-revolution will not be televised.

Start now, as soon as you put down this book. Life is an adventure, and it's later then you think. So, let's be on our way.

Reactionary Leaders

From English kings to American presidents, from anarcho-monarchists to Anti-Federalists, the reactionary has no shortage of role models in the political sphere. These are men who sought to preserve the balance between charity and independence, and to maintain the harmony between freedom and duty.

It's an eclectic group, to be sure, and I don't know that any of them would fit the definition of a model reactionary. But there's something to learn from each of them, and each in his own way has made his mark on the reactionary mind.

Edward the Confessor (1003–1066). Pious, chaste, and ineffectual. The model ruler.

Richard III (1452–1485). A brave and chivalrous man who died opposing that depraved social climber Henry Tudor. The last king of England to die in battle.

Girolamo Savonarola (1452–1498). Italian art critic and religious thinker who vigorously campaigned against the Medicis' exploitation of the Florentine poor.

Thomas More (1478–1535). The most learned man of his age, who gave his life defending the sanctity of marriage. A self-made man and friend of the poor, as well as a prolific burner of heretics.

John Winthrop (1587–1649). An intrepid pilgrim and moderate Puritan who sought to found New England as a "model of charity."

Charles I (1600–1649). A just and holy king. Executed for his defense of the common man against the ambitions of the squirearchy. A martyr of the Church of England against the dour Presbyterians.

James II (1633–1701). The last Catholic king of England. Deposed in favor of William and Mary, who ushered in such "reforms" as the Atlantic slave trade, a standing army, and the supremacy of an oligarchical Parliament.

Junípero Serra (1713–1784). The "Apostle of California" and Inquisitor of New Spain. Extended the borders of Christendom to the West Coast of North America. Promoted the rights of indigenous people.

Joshua Atherton (1737–1809). Early New Hampshire statesman who advocated both for states' rights and the abolition of slavery.

Thomas Jefferson (1743–1826). Progenitor of the American localist, agrarian tradition. Strident opponent of Big Government and Big Business... at least until he became president.

John Adams (1735–1826). The founding father most dedicated to America's Christian character. Author of the Massachusetts Constitution, which calls for public worship and state-sponsored religious education. Openly admired the feudal monarchs who defended the peasantry against bankers, traders, and landlords.

William Cobbett (1763–1835). Agrarian pamphleteer and member of Parliament for the Radical Party. Campaigned vigorously for the rights of farmers and small landholders. Stridently opposed both the growing bureaucracy and the bloated financial elite. Leading advocate for Catholic Emancipation.

John Randolph of Roanoke (1773–1833). Virginia senator who resisted centralization both in politics and economics. "I am an aristocrat," he declared. "I love liberty, I hate equality."

Andrew Jackson (1767–1845). Championed family farms and small businesses against "modernizing" oligarchs who sought cooperation between government, finance, and industry.

Franklin Pierce (1804–1869). According to Russell Kirk, "an intelligent, moderate, and honest gentleman of considerable talents with whom partisan historians have dealt brutally."

Benjamin Disraeli (1804–1881). British prime minister for the Conservative Party. Led the "Young England" movement, which sought to rally the old aristocracy and peasantry against the ascendant bourgeoisie. The first real neo-feudalist in Anglo-American history. Founder of the one-nation school of Toryism.

Leo XIII (1810–1903). Philosopher-pope who restored solidarity and subsidiarity to the heart of Christian political thought. His encyclical *Rerum Novarum* was the chief inspiration for distributism.

Lord Salisbury (1830–1903). Prime minister for the Conservative Party who declared, "Whatever happens will be for the worse, and therefore it is in our interest that as little should happen as possible."

Theodore Roosevelt (1858–1919). Distinguished statesman, soldier, hunter, author, polyglot, naturalist, and conservationist. Sought to break up corporate monopolies, support working families, preserve American agriculture, and defend our natural resources. Promoted the "strenuous life" and embodied the spirit of rugged individualism.

William Jennings Bryan (1860–1925). Tribune of the plebs, anti-imperialist, and staunch anti-Darwinist. What's not to love?

Hilaire Belloc (1870–1953). Distributist writer and member of Parliament for the Liberal Party. During one of his stump speeches, he was jeered for being a "papist." Belloc replied by taking his prayer beads out of his pocket and cried, "Gentlemen, I am a Catholic. As far as possible, I go to Mass every day. This is a rosary. As far as possible, I kneel down and tell these beads every day. If you reject me on account of my religion, I shall thank God that He has spared me the indignity of being your representative."

António de Oliveira Salazar (1889–1970). Portuguese strongman who extolled "the intrinsic value of religious truth to the individual and society" and lamented that "politics killed administration."

Dorothy Day (1897–1980). Her potent blend of anarchism and distributism evolved into a program for radical, grassroots social reform—one firmly grounded in Christian orthodoxy.

Roger Scruton (1944–2020). Conservative philosopher and chairman of Britain's "Building Better, Building Beautiful Commission," which is devoted to restoring a traditional aesthetic in British public architecture.

Viktor Orbán (1963–). A self-professed "illiberal" conservative who uses state power to squelch LGBT propaganda, incentivize large families, and preserve Hungary's Christian character. A staunch opponent of progressive plutocrats, and a stauncher proponent of economic localism.

Reactionary Pastimes

Human beings aren't made to be sedentary—physically, mentally, or spiritually. That's just not how we're built. And yet both our work and our leisure are dominated by drudgery. Many of us want to break free from the tedium of modern life, but we don't even know where to begin.

First, ditch the smartphone. Smash the TV. Cancel your subscriptions to *Men's Health* and *People*. You can't build a garden unless you clear out the weeds first.

Second, I recommend "The Strenuous Life": a program run by the folks behind the blog *The Art of Manliness*. It begins with a three-month boot camp designed to kick-start your body, mind, and soul. The Strenuous Life program is built on that reactionary maxim: that a man is strong *so he can be useful*.

Beyond that, here are a few more suggestions for work and leisure:

FITNESS

Walking
Hiking
Rucking
Hunting
Fishing

Bird-watching

Archery

Swimming (ideally, in a natural body of water)

Sailing, canoeing, and related activities

Horseback riding

Camping

Traditional martial arts, such as boxing and fencing

"Woodsmen Workouts": strength training with objects found in nature

Gardening (if only a couple of tomato plants by a window)

Raising livestock (it's surprisingly easy to keep chickens!)

LEISURE

Chess

Card games (besides poker)

Writing letters

Writing poetry

Journaling

Whittling

Beekeeping

Beer-brewing

Furniture-making

Canning

Cooking

Sewing (a very useful skill)

Storytelling

Painting

Taxidermy

Meditation

Model trains

Playing music
Dancing
Smoking
Parlor games (such as Charades)
Horseshoes (cornhole for grown-ups)

NO-NOS

"Ball sports": Geoffroi de Charny says they're the domain of women and were taken over by men too lazy or scared to joust.

Weightlifting: a waste of time and energy.

Wine-tasting: a waste of good wine.

Travel: Taking selfies in a different city isn't interesting or sophisticated. Unless you're sumo wrestling in Japan or hunting lions in Africa, stay home and get a real hobby.

Slam poetry: not poetry.

Shopping: if you can afford to shop just for fun, you have too much money.

Gastronomy: Cooking is an art. Eating is not.

Yoga: unless you happen to be Hindu.

Video games: good lord.

Skateboarding and snowboarding.

Reactionary Dogs

Most dog breeds are good for something.

Odds are, deep within that little furball sleeping on your feet, lurks the soul of a cold-blooded killer. Virtually every large- to medium-sized dog in the United States was bred to hunt something. For some, it might be bears; for others, it could be mice. But real dogs like to kill things. Some are happy to herd, such as the gentle Pyrenees, which will kill a coyote that tries to abscond with its sheep.

Discovering the original use of these dog breeds is fascinating in itself. But I hope this list will also be helpful to anyone looking to buy a dog. Dogs make the best pets (except maybe pigs, which turn your food scraps into delicious bacon). If you're going to buy a dog, though, please put it to good use. If you want to buy a chocolate lab, take up duck hunting. If you want a dachshund, get a taste for possum meat.

But, please, don't get a dog just to have him sit around the house. People even train their dogs not to bark at squirrels who run around outside. *That's their job*. It'd be like lining a little boy's room with toy guns, foam swords, and action figures…and then telling him he can't play with any of them. No, Billy. Shhhh. Don't ask again or I'll hit you with this newspaper.

Folks, that's not love. Owning a dog is a two-way street. They'll give you unconditional love and obedience; you owe them more than a bowl of Purina once or twice a day.

You'll find all sorts of lists on the internet for "home alone" breeds: dogs that are supposedly well-suited to owners who are going to be away from home most of the day. Let's be clear: there are no "home alone" dogs. Dogs are pack animals. They don't like to be shut up in a house all day by themselves. As a rule of thumb—and there are basically no exceptions—always own at least two dogs. At least. More is always better. If you can't afford more than one dog, your dog can't afford you. If you don't have enough room for two dogs, you don't have enough room for one.

Do the research. Border Collies get especially lonesome, particularly when they don't get enough exercise. Lassie is the very last dog you want to leave in the apartment for nine or ten hours a day.

Below is a list of common dog breeds and what they were originally bred for. Now, this list is far from extensive, and many breeds are surprisingly versatile. (Dachshunds are pretty good at tracking deer.) Do some research. But this list should at least get the gears turning. When you buy a dog, make sure it's a good fit for you—and, just as important, make sure *you're* a good fit for *him*.

USEFUL DOG BREEDS AND THEIR USES

Golden Retriever: bird hunting
Labrador Retriever: bird hunting
Chesapeake Bay Retriever: bird hunting
Brittany: bird hunting
German Shepherd: home defense, herding
Doberman: home defense
Mastiff: home defense

Border Collie: herding
Great Pyrenees: livestock guardian
Bernese Mountain Dog: herding, drafting
Rottweiler: home defense, herding, drafting
Whippet: hunting small game, especially rabbit
Redbone Coonhound: racoon hunting
Jack Russell Terrier: foxhunting
Terriers: pest control, especially rats
Foxhound: deer hunting, foxhunting
Pitbull: hunting large game
Boxer: hunting large game
Dachshund: pest control, especially badgers and mice
English Pointer: pointing (birds)
Irish Setter: setting (birds)
Beagle: beagling (hares/rabbits)

USELESS DOG BREEDS THAT SHOULDN'T EXIST

Pug
Pomeranian
Chihuahua
Shih Tzu
Bijon Frise
Papillon
Pekingese
Anything that ends in -doodle

Reactionary Drinks

As Ben Shapiro once wrote: "Whiskey tastes like turpentine. All who pretend otherwise may be safely categorized with those who say that they just *love* salad.... No sane person prefers whiskey to a strawberry daiquiri." As usual, Mr. Shapiro was wrong.

When it comes to adult beverages, there are three basic reactionary schools of thought.

The first—which we'll call the Simpleton School—was laid out by Chesterton and Belloc, who refused to drink anything invented after the Reformation. This, to their mind, meant limiting themselves to beer and wine. They apparently didn't consider that many popular liquors, like gin, were distilled by monks and sold as medicinal tonics long before Martin Luther reared his ugly head. But there's a certain rugged nobility in refusing to take strong drink, and I wouldn't discourage anyone who chooses to follow their example.

The second, the Purist School, accepts hard spirits but rejects cocktails. Cocktails are a uniquely American invention. They came into vogue during Prohibition: bootleggers cut their bathtub spirits with orange juice to hide the noxious flavor. Again, I won't disagree with those reactionaries who only take straight whiskey. But I don't share their prejudice.

The third, the Universalist School, will take anything that's offered to them. Though I generally stick to beer myself, I'm a Universalist on principle. Usually, I'm happy to drink anything that's at least 5 percent alcohol by volume...so long as it isn't too fruity.

And so, here's a handy guide to the most reactionary cocktails of all time.

Martini

You'll have heard a lot of smarmy nonsense about the "right" way to make a martini. Some argue that we've deviated from the original recipe: that we no longer use enough vermouth, or that we ought to use a lemon twist, or that it should be stirred and *not* shaken.

Don't listen to them. The reactionary knows that just because something happens to be older doesn't mean that it's *necessarily* better. Granted, usually it will be. But let me assure you, dear reader, that there's no "right" way to make a martini. It's a matter of what tastes best.

However, the reactionary also knows that taste isn't subjective. While there might not be a "right" way to make a martini, there is a *best* way. Here's the recipe for the best possible martini.

1. Fill cocktail shaker with ice.
2. Rinse cocktail shaker with vermouth.
3. Strain out vermouth.
4. Add three shots of gin and one dash of olive juice.
5. Shake gently.
6. Garnish with olive.

There's a question of what gin to use. I prefer Gordon's—which, for years, was preferred by everyone in England, from the country squires to the inner-city fishwives. Second would be Bombay (not Bombay Sapphire, just Bombay), followed by Tanqueray.

The kind of olives is a variable. I recommend you buy feta-stuffed and wrap them in anchovies. Perfection.

Gin and Tonic

2 parts gin
3 parts tonic water
1/6 lime, squeezed

The gin and tonic is the perfect year-round cocktail. Sitting on the porch in the heat of summer, it's the perfect drink to cool the brow. Smoking pipes by the woodstove in the dead of winter, it's the perfect drink to cool the tongue.

The reactionary will always opt for Gordon's gin, which was ubiquitous in the Royal Navy when the gin and tonic was invented; Gordon's was almost certainly used in the first 100,000 G&Ts made across the British Empire. He will also use a superior tonic water like Fentimans, which doesn't contain high-fructose corn syrup.

Chartreuse and Tonic

2 parts Chartreuse
3 parts tonic water
No garnish

While both gin and Chartreuse were developed by medieval monks, gin (and especially gin and tonics) have come to be associated with Britain's Anglican gentry. So, you might say the Chartreuse and tonic is the Catholic G&T. I also happen to think it tastes a whole lot better. It's not as light, and you can't knock back four or five in quick succession...but then, that might be a virtue. And the robust flavor more than makes up for it. Just try it before you knock it.

Pink Gin

3 shots of gin
6 dashes of bitters
1 cocktail onion

The Pink Gin is a breakfast cocktail: Evelyn Waugh drank one every morning with his newspaper. Despite the witheringly high alcohol content, to consume a Pink Gin at any other time of day will correctly lead to accusations of being a sissy.

The Bonnie Prince

3 parts champagne
2 parts St.-Germain

This is an old mixture, but it doesn't have a proper name, so I'm giving it one. It's named after the manliest man ever to be called "Bonnie." He was a dashing young aristocrat for whom thousands of rugged, illiterate Scottish peasants gave their lives. He is, in short, a reactionary icon.

The Bonnie Prince is a deceptively delicate drink. Elderflower liqueur is botanical, yet light and smooth. It's sweet, but not *too* sweet. It's a great drink for picnics and garden parties. And it will be loved by the burliest gents and the daintiest of ladies—just like the Young Pretender.

Mint Julep

The mint julep perfectly distills the essence of Southern Agrari-anism into a highball glass. Not being a Southerner myself, I've taken a survey of my friends below the Mason-Dixon on how to make it right. They all agree that Walker Percy gave the best recipe of all time in his 1975 essay "Bourbon":

> You need excellent Bourbon whiskey; rye or Scotch will not do. Put half an inch of sugar in the bottom of glass and merely dampen it with water. Next, very quickly—and here is the trick in the procedure—crush your ice, actually pow-der it, preferably in a towel with a wooden mallet, so quickly that it remains dry, and, slipping two sprigs of fresh mint against the inside of the glass, cram the ice right to the brim, packing it with your hand. Finally, fill the glass, which apparently has no room left for anything else, with Bourbon, the older the better, and grate a bit of nutmeg on the top. The glass will frost immediately. Then settle back in your chair for half an hour of cumulative bliss.

A little complex but, when done right, drinking is always a Patient Art.

Reactionary Books (Non-Fiction)

A s a reactionary, I must urge you *not* to read any books on political philosophy. They're full of boring, ridiculous theories about which writers have no business theorizing. You won't learn anything from them except how to be vain and unhappy.

Having said that, if one absolutely insists on reading about politics, here's a list of books that fall broadly into the reactionary school of political philosophy. Of course, no such school really exists. That is our pride and glory. So, the list will be eclectic.

Most of these books I've quoted in *The Reactionary Mind*. All of them have influenced my thinking in one way or another. I'll break them into three categories.

The first is "Medieval and Medievalist." These are books that are written about, during, or in defense of the Middle Ages. The second is "Counter-Revolutionary." These are all European, and all are responding to some ongoing revolution in politics or society. This is the real meat of what's usually known as reactionary political philosophy, but I think it's also the least relevant to modern audiences. The third I'm calling "Restorationist." These are modern writers in the Anglo-American tradition who are trying to rediscover some long-lost truths or to resurrect the natural order of things.

The fourth, I think, is the most important. These are our guides to "Reactionary Living." They teach us to reclaim the wisdom of tradition in order to defend ourselves against the stultifying effects of modern life. They're sort of like far-right self-help books. If you have to read any nonfiction, I strongly suggest you begin with these. Enjoy.

I. Medieval and Medievalist

The Portable Medieval Reader published by Penguin
The City of God by Augustine of Hippo
Policraticus by John of Salisbury
The Book of the Order of Chivalry by Raymond Llull
A Knight's Own Book of Chivalry by Geffroi de Charny
Utopia by Thomas More
Politics Drawn from Holy Scripture by Jacques-Bénigne Bossuet
Medieval Essays by Christopher Dawson
Those Terrible Middle Ages! by Régine Pernoud
God's Battalions by Rodney Stark

II. Counter-Revolutionary

De Monarchia by Dante Alighieri
Patriarcha by Robert Filmer
The True Law of Free Monarchies by James VI and I
The Idea of the Patriot King by Lord Bolingbroke
The True and Only Wealth of Nations by Louis de Bonald
Considerations on France by Joseph de Maistre
The Genius of Christianity by François-René de Chateaubriand
The Liberal Illusion by Louis Veuillot
Liberalism by Louis Billot, S.J.
Authority, Liberty, and Function by Ramiro de Maeztu
The Crisis of Western Philosophy by Vladimir Solovyov
Catholic Political Thought, 1789–1848 edited by Bela Menczer

Critics of the Enlightenment edited by Christopher Blum

The French Right, From Maistre to Maurras edited by J. S. McClelland

III. Restorationist

Young England: The New Generation edited by John Morrow

Rural Rides by William Cobbett

The Servile State by Hilaire Belloc

What's Wrong With the World by G. K. Chesterton

Nazareth or Social Chaos by Fr. Vincent McNabb

Progress and Poverty by Henry George

Land and Liberty: The Best of Free America edited by Allan C. Carlson

I'll Take My Stand by the Twelve Southerners

The Dynamics of World History by Christopher Dawson

Land! by John Crowe Ransom

Leisure, the Basis of Culture by Josef Pieper

Why Work? by Dorothy L. Sayers

Liberty or Equality by Erik von Kuehnelt-Leddihn

Christianity and Culture by T. S. Eliot

Enemies of the Permanent Things by Russell Kirk

Small Is Beautiful by E. F. Schumacher

The Restoration of Christian Culture by John Senior

After Virtue by Alasdair MacIntyre

The Realm by Aidan Nichols, O.P.

Statecraft as Soulcraft by George F. Will

The Unsettling of America by Wendell Berry

Fields Without Dreams by Victor Davis Hanson

Look Homeward, America by Bill Kauffman

The Two-Income Trap by Elizabeth Warren and Amelia Warren Tyagi

The Abolition of Britain by Peter Hitchens

Grand New Party by Ross Douthat and Reihan Salam
The Prodigal Church by Brandon McGinley
Liberal Shock edited by William Dawes

IV. Reactionary Living

The Rule of St. Benedict by Benedict of Nursia
Handbook of a Christian Knight by Desiderius Erasmus
Walden by Henry David Thoreau
The Strenuous Life by Theodore Roosevelt
The Young Fogey Handbook by Suzanne Lowry
The Hour: A Cocktail Manifesto by Bernard DeVoto
The Foxfire Book by Eliot Wigginton
Hallowed Be This House by Thomas Howard
On Hunting by Roger Scruton
Robert E. Lee on Leadership by H. W. Crocker III
Last Child in the Woods by Richard Louv
Shop Class as Soulcraft by Matthew Crawford
Folks, This Ain't Normal by Joel Salatin
The Benedict Option by Rod Dreher
The Power of Silence by Cardinal Robert Sarah
12 Rules for Life by Jordan Peterson
Stop Reading the News by Rolf Dobelli
The Art of Manliness by Brett McKay

Reactionary Books (Literature)

Here's a list of good books to read *and enjoy*. They're not the books you *should* read (according to some highbrow). They're not "teachable." They're just good. Most of them will instruct; some will edify; but all will entertain.

I've begun with a few volumes of children's literature, and I heartily implore my reader to do the same. If you're going to give yourself a proper education, you must begin at the beginning. It's amazing how a good children's book can awaken and excite the imagination. Even if you (like me) are a grown-up and have spent your life reading trash, these little books will coax your mind open. The perfect reactionary would read nothing but good children's literature, and he'd be a better man for it. If you haven't read them yet, do so at once. Put down this dreary tome and get yourself a copy of *Winnie-the-Pooh*.

Needless to say, the list isn't exhaustive. I've tried to recommend only one volume per author. (One must make exceptions for a man like Tolkien.) But read everything by each of them, if you can.

There are plenty of dry books that one would do well to read, like Cardinal Newman's *Apologia*. But these days I almost refuse to pick up anything that isn't funny, spooky, or action-packed. There's enough tragedy in life; one needn't add to it by reading *King Lear*. A man's library should be there to cheer him up at the end of a long day.

The poetry is all formalist; it's written in rhyme and meter. I make no apology for that. Like everything else, poetry ought to be formal.

Masters of "free verse" such as T. S. Eliot are only exceptions that prove the rule. Free verse (or informalism) on the whole tends to be lazy, stupid, and ugly. Not one in a million can do it well, and it might be best if we stopped trying.

This catalogue will also arm you with references you can deploy at cocktail parties with the literati, should you find yourself in such unfortunate circumstances. If you can talk intelligently about even four or five of them, you'll have the upper hand on almost any living holder of a bachelor of arts degree.

CHILDREN'S BOOKS

Winnie-the-Pooh by A. A. Milne

The Wind in the Willows by Kenneth Grahame

The Secret Garden by Frances Hodgson Burnett

The Selfish Giant by Oscar Wilde

Irish Folk and Fairy Tales by W. B. Yeats

The Princess and the Goblin by George MacDonald

Cautionary Tales for Children by Hilaire Belloc

The Chronicles of Narnia by C. S. Lewis

The Prince and the Pauper by Mark Twain

NOVELS

Sir Gawain and the Green Knight translated by J. R. R. Tolkien

Frankenstein by Mary Shelley

The Hobbit by J. R. R. Tolkien

Lord of the Rings by J. R. R. Tolkien

A Connecticut Yankee in King Arthur's Court by Mark Twain

Twenty Thousand Leagues Under the Sea by Jules Verne

King Solomon's Mines by H. Rider Haggard
Strange Case of Dr. Jekyll and Mr. Hyde by Robert Lewis Stevenson
The Three Musketeers by Alexandre Dumas
The Scarlet Pimpernel by the Baroness Orczy
Riders of the Purple Sage by Zane Grey
Manalive by G. K. Chesterton
And Then There Were None by Agatha Christie
Brideshead Revisited by Evelyn Waugh
Whose Body? by Dorothy L. Sayers
Paying Guests by E. F. Benson
Three Men and a Boat by Jerome K. Jerome
Greenmantle by John Buchan
Dracula by Bram Stoker
Lost Horizons by James Hilton
Old House of Fear by Russell Kirk
The Old Limey by H. W. Crocker III

SHORT STORIES

The *Sketch Book* stories of Washington Irving
The *Father Brown* stories of G. K. Chesterton
The *Sherlock Holmes* stories of Sir Arthur Conan Doyle
The *Jeeves and Wooster* stories of P. G. Wodehouse
The satires of Saki (H. H. Munro)
The ghost stories of M. R. James
The Cthulhu stories of H. P. Lovecraft
The stories of Edgar Allan Poe

POETRY & POETS

The Iliad by Homer
The Aeneid by Virgil
Beowulf translated by Seamus Heaney
Canterbury Tales by Geoffrey Chaucer
Paradise by Dante Alighieri[1]
Hebrew Melodies by Lord Byron
Old Possum's Book of Practical Cats by T. S. Eliot
W. B. Yeats
Gerard Manley Hopkins
Robert Burns
Robert Frost
W. H. Auden
John Betjeman
R. S. Thomas

HISTORY

The Lives by Plutarch
The Cyropedia by Xenophon
The Histories by Herodotus
The Conspiracy of Catiline by Sallust
Le Morte d'Arthur by Sir Thomas Mallory
Ecclesiastical History of the English People by Bede
The Education of Henry Adams by Henry Adams
St. Francis of Assisi by Michael de la Bédoyère
The Greeks by H. D. F. Kitto
A Colder Eye by Hugh Kenner

PHILOSOPHY

The sayings of Diogenes
The Republic by Plato
On Duties by Cicero
Meditations by Marcus Aurelius
The Consolation of Philosophy by Boethius
Utopia by Thomas More
In Praise of Folly by Erasmus
The Soul of Man Under Socialism by Oscar Wilde
Orthodoxy by G. K. Chesterton
Leisure: The Basis of Culture by Josef Pieper

Acknowledgments

First and foremost, I'd like to thank all the good folks at Regnery, especially Tom Spence and Harry Crocker. They've gone above and beyond their duties of an editor and publisher and become advocates, advisors, and friends. They certainly went out on a limb with this book. I hope I do them justice.

I'd also like to thank all of the friends and colleagues who made this book possible, including Dominic Cassella, Dr. Marek Chodakiewicz, Sir Charles Coulombe, David Counts, William Dawes, Rod Dreher, Dr. Amy Fahey, Dr. William Fahey, Clark Ingram, Annette Kirk, Oliver J. J. Lane, Matt Purple, James Vogel, Fr. George Rutler, Roger Tindall, and Michael Yost. There are too many others to name, and some who prefer not to be named at all. But they know who they are, and they have my sincere gratitude.

Also my parents, who have always been my biggest (and, perhaps, my only) fans. From the bottom of my heart, thank you, and I love you.

My best man, Alexander Horan, who taught me everything I know about being a reactionary.

My daughter, Beatrice—the littlest peanut, the light of my life.

And, of course, Helena: my beautiful, kind, intelligent, and long-suffering wife. Everything I do is for her, and without her I could do nothing.

Ad maiorem Dei gloriam.

Notes

Chapter Three: Why the Reactionary Has a Sneaking Suspicion for Savonarola

1. Eastern Christians have persistently rejected "realism" in their religious art (especially iconography) for just this reason. See especially *Christ Pantocrator.*

Chapter Four: Why Reactionaries Defend the Inquisition

1. Rod Dreher has chronicled the rise of a new caste of self-appointed progressive censors in his brilliant book *Live Not by Lies.*

Chapter Five: Why Reactionaries Don't "Follow the Science"

1. As it happens, some true experts doubt the established theories as well. Professor John Peebles, an astrophysicist who won the 2019 Nobel Prize in Physics, thinks the Big Bang is bunk. "It connotes the notion of an event and a position, both of which are quite wrong," he insists. "It's very unfortunate that one thinks of the beginning whereas in fact, we have no good theory of such a thing as the beginning."
2. The persistence of faith also pains the Deweyites, which is why they slander poor Bellarmine.

Chapter Six: Why Reactionaries Don't Worship Reason

1. A prominent and highly intelligent conservative commentator recently pointed this out, in a somewhat different way, and the military responded—with a hissy fit.

2. Three thousand souls were executed by the Spanish Inquisition over three and a half centuries, or about eight per annum. The state of Texas executed 563 people between 1982 and 2019, or about fifteen per annum.

Chapter Seven: Why a Reactionary Would Like to Abolish Politics

1. Chamber pots were themselves not entirely en vogue. Several firsthand accounts of life in Versailles attest to the fact that the upper gentry felt themselves above such inconvenience as relieving themselves in a small metal basin. Instead, they would pass water freely in the hallways and let the servants clean it up.

Chapter Nine: The Reactionary American

1. That was the same Mr. Lincoln who referred to Franklin Pierce as a "wicked free-soiler" before succeeding him as president.

Chapter Fifteen: Technoholics Anonymous

1. It's also why tech gurus such as Bill Gates and Steve Jobs refused to let their kids use smartphones until they were well into their teens. Hint-hint.

Chapter Sixteen: The Patient Arts

1. I've written *The Reactionary Mind* assuming that only men will read it. Most women have more sense than to pick up a book with a picture of a bowler hat and a monocle on the cover.

2. For the definitive treatment of this subject, see "Tobacco and the Soul" by Michael P. Foley (*First Things*, April 1997).

3. If this seems too dainty for you, I understand; we'll soon get to the advantages of drinking beer in the morning.
4. Also see *The Market Gardener: A Successful Grower's Handbook for Small-Scale Organic Farming* by Jean-Martin Fortier.

Chapter Seventeen: Musings of a Human Liberationist
1. "The earth brought forth vegetation, plants yielding seed according to their own kinds, and trees bearing fruit in which is their seed, each according to its kind. And God saw that it was good" (Genesis 1:12).
2. "Let us make man in our image, after our likeness; and let them have dominion over the fish of the sea, and over the birds of the air, and over the cattle, and over all the earth, and over every creeping thing that creeps upon the earth" (Genesis 1:26).

Chapter Eighteen: The Strenuous Life
1. Ice-fishing excepted.

Conclusion: The Coming Dark Age
1. Ideally, of course, it would be handled for us by our king!

Appendix Six: Reactionary Books (Literature)
1. Only the most devoted Danteans should read the *Inferno* and *Purgatorio*.

Index